THE BIRTH OF A NEW WORKFORCE

21st-Century Strategies That Will Revolutionize Your Business

Randall W. Hatcher

Pursuit Books

Augusta, Georgia

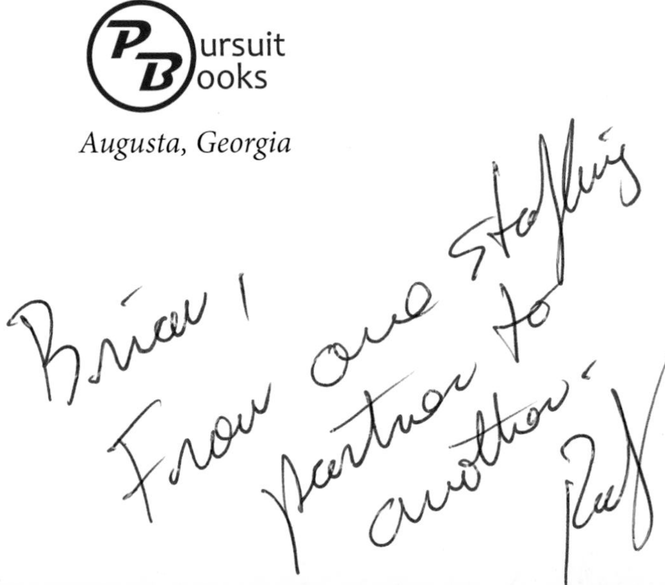

Published by Pursuit Books
501 Greene Street
Augusta, GA 30901
www.PursuitBooks.com

Editorial: Sandra Jonas
Book Design: Mike Friehauf

Contributors:
Jeff Owens, President, Advanced Technology Services
Vince Sparrow, Senior Managing Director, Outsourced Partners International

Publisher's Cataloging-in-Publication Data

Hatcher, Randall W.
The birth of a new workforce : 21st-century strategies that will revolutionize your business / Randall W. Hatcher.
Augusta, GA : Pursuit Books, c2011.

p. : ill. ; cm.

ISBN: 9780982793350
ISBN: 9780982793381 (deluxe)

1. Human capital - Management. 2. Strategic planning. 3. Contracting out

HF5549 .H38 2011 658.3—dc22

2010932905

This edition is printed on acid-free paper.

In loving memory of my mother

Marion Harris Hatcher

who always saw the best in me

and taught me to laugh

Contents

Acknowledgments

Few people have the opportunities I had growing up in a successful family business. My father, William G. Hatcher Sr., deserves my deepest gratitude for believing in me and giving me a chance straight out of the University of Georgia in 1978. Thank you, Dad.

I have enjoyed the rare privilege of working with a dedicated group of employees at MAU (Management, Analysis, and Utilization Inc.). I want to single out my assistant, Barbara Lowe, who not only is extremely competent but also has stayed with me for twenty-five years. She has helped me transcribe and edit thousands of communications into meaningful exchanges that have improved relationships both inside and outside our company. Most importantly, she helped me finish this book.

I also owe much gratitude to Ed Knapp, who turned a crisis in 1987 into MAU's first outsourcing opportunity. He showed me how we could expand our vision by offering much more to our customers than just recruiting and staffing commodity services.

I would like to express my full appreciation to our loyal customers, many of whose real-life stories are illustrated in this book and stand as excellent models for teaching all of us how to run a better company.

My association with the Young Presidents' Organization has stretched me in so many ways. I am particularly grateful for the Ramey Forum and offer a special thanks to forum-mate Frank Buonanotte for encouraging me to write this book.

Finally, my wife of over thirty-one years has loved me more than any man deserves. A brilliant woman, she could have done anything professionally. She chose instead to provide me the freedom to focus on the business during its critical years while she assumed the more important role of raising our three children, Adam, Baker, and Anne Randall. *The two shall become one* describes the miracle we live together every day. I am truly blessed. I love you, Marilee.

Never Waste a Crisis

Congratulations! If you're reading this, you are probably part of that small group of business leaders who have survived (at least so far) the greatest recession in over twenty-five years. That's the good news. The bad news is that your competitors are also reading this. They're survivors too, and when things turn around, they will use what they've learned during this down economy to try to put you out of business. Smarter and more capitalized, they'll be seeking the chance to grow at a record pace by taking advantage of what in many cases is a smaller commercial landscape.

What have *you* learned? What are you going to do differently in the future? A friend of mine who works for an international aluminum smelter told me that every Friday for most of 2009, corporate headquarters had a conference call with all their plants to announce which ones were closing. Every week, he sat on that call and held his breath knowing that his plant could be the next one on the chopping block. Fortunately for him, that didn't happen, and out of his pain came a valuable revelation, which you'll discover in the pages ahead.

Never in any of our careers has there been a better time to consider new ways to operate our businesses and, in my context here, to consider new workforce concepts and partnership models. Never has there been a better time to pursue these ideas with a "no sacred cows" mentality.

For thirty-seven years, our company, MAU, has helped local, national, and international organizations change the way they ***m***anage, ***a***nalyze, and ***u***tilize their workforce. Since I joined the company in 1978, we have provided employment opportunities for more than 500,000 people domestically and globally, from the janitor to the president, for a day, a week —or forever.

From this vantage point, I have accumulated over three decades' worth of proven solutions for transforming companies and making them more competitive, many of which I propose in this book. Although manufacturers make up my target audience, if you're an executive in any type of business, you'll find plenty of meaty ideas to chew on. Some of them might seem radical—too much of a departure from your old business blueprint—but I guarantee that if you take the chance and implement at least one new concept, your future will be the better for it.

I begin with a history of the American workforce and then move into the specific ways you can redesign your business to position it for success in the twenty-first century. You'll find insights and practical tools, including a number of graphs, diagrams, and process flowcharts that you can quickly modify to fit your needs.

Companies differ in many ways, from their products and services to their cultures, yet they all have two things in common: (1) a set of defining characteristics—those that distinguish them from their competitors; and (2) the "other stuff"—the functions, processes, and responsibilities that have little to do with what an organization is known for but still absorb a great deal of time and resources.

I hope this book will inspire you to take a serious look at both areas and change the way you manage your business. Further, I'd like to challenge you to consider new strategies to ensure that you disproportionately benefit from the anticipated upturn in the economy.

And when times do improve—when the layoffs, plant closings, and bankruptcies are behind us—put what you learned to good use. Indeed, remember to follow a favorite maxim of mine: "Never waste a crisis."

ONE

How Good Is Great?

Golf professional Kenny Perry was leading the 2009 Masters Golf Tournament in Augusta, Georgia, on the final day with two holes to go. At age forty-eight, he had worked all his golfing life for this moment: a chance to win a major tournament. His second shot on the seventeenth hole ended up on the back fringe of the green, leaving him a difficult but very playable chip shot. Unfortunately, though, his next shot landed too far from the hole for him to make par. He bogeyed instead, a one-stroke mistake that ultimately cost him the championship.

During an interview later, a reporter asked Kenny what happened on hole seventeen. He said something to the effect that really great players would have made the shot, so maybe he wasn't that great a player. I have to admit that his words saddened me. Here was a dedicated, longtime professional questioning his abilities. He had made it to the big dance, to the pinnacle of his career, and yet he'd failed.

I believe we can learn something from Kenny Perry's experience: just like great people, great companies can fail—even at the height of their success. Businesses can go under for a variety of reasons, but I predict that in the future, those achieving longevity will be run by leaders who understand they cannot be great unless every position in the company is being managed with excellence, from the janitor all the way up to the CEO.

I encourage you to begin exploring the "what ifs" of your company. I'd like to unlock your thinking to consider how you can better focus on the parts of your business that will ensure long-term success.

Takeaway

- Past greatness does not guarantee a company's future.
- In the years to come, thriving businesses will know how to manage every part of their organization with excellence.
- The most successful executives will concentrate a majority of their time and resources on what will keep their companies growing and prospering in the decades ahead.

TWO

It Could Happen to You

Ray Meads was the VP of Butler Manufacturing, a division of the Pisces Group. He had risen swiftly through the ranks of this international giant by taking advantage of the parent company's financial strength as it acquired competitors, which in turn provided him greater opportunities.

This climb had continued for two decades, and now at the age of forty-five, Ray was beginning to realize that he had been blinded by the intoxicating pace and rewards of his corporate ascension. Although what he had been doing for years in building new plants and rolling up competitors had undoubtedly proved successful, something had changed along the way.

In the current marketplace, he needed to evaluate how his business model had eroded. You see, Ray had been reading from the old *labor blueprint* from which many other executives are still reading today. They keep doing things the same way, sticking to their knitting. After all, it's always worked in the past.

Yes, Ray had contracted out the low-hanging fruit of standard corporate functions—security, janitorial, trucking, food service, and landscaping. But inside the plant, where his products were made, lived the sacred cows: the full-time employees who managed the manufacturing and support processes. Occasionally, Ray called in a small percentage of temporary help for peaks and special projects. However, in the end, he was absorbing the impact of the long-term, fixed labor costs of his plants. Even after driving down his inventory and raw material costs as far as he could, he was becoming less competitive not only with his rivals but also with his own company's sister plants.

Ray needed to find a partner with some new ideas—and he didn't have much time.

Takeaways

- Have you made many business changes over the years but found your market share still slipping?
- Are you constantly making excuses to avoid addressing the high price tag and inefficiencies of your full-time regular workforce?
- Are you afraid to eliminate any of your sacred cows?

THREE

The Corporate Family

What a great country the United States is. Early business pioneers perhaps understood this best—the Rockefellers, Carnegies, and Fords. They participated in the U.S. manufacturing transformation that would ultimately produce more than one-third of all global industrial output.

Between the late-eighteenth and early-twentieth centuries, America gave birth to many of the world's most successful companies. From these came second-, third-, and fourth-generation international entities and spinoffs. In most of these organizations, everyone worked for the "Company": one big, happy "Family" of full-time regular employees—the janitors, cafeteria workers, security guards, groundskeepers, drivers, managers, and CEO. They all belonged to the Family and they all received a paycheck from the Company. According to this **Patriarchal Workforce Model**, people expected to stay with one organization until they retired—or died.

Over time, many of the Family members grew dissatisfied, maybe because of too much perceived or actual corporate greed, too much concentration of power and money, or too much employee abuse. Eager to improve their situation, some of these disenfranchised workers sought the help of an outside partner: the union.

Unionized companies provided higher pay scales and rich benefits, including health care and generous retirement programs (which eventally became too generous). Whether or not you support unions, you can't question their significant influence on wages and benefits throughout the marketplace, since even the nonunion companies copied from union playbooks. In many cases, they did so just to make sure they kept the unions out. Although businesses didn't particularly like the situation, corporate profits were soaring, and there seemed to be enough money to go around for everyone.

Patriarchal Workforce Model:

A big Family of full-time regular employees working for one Company their entire lives

With its static full-time workforce, the Patriarchal Model offered no buffer against changing business conditions, seasonality, or market fluctuations. Consequently, as figure 1 illustrates, companies found themselves overstaffed when their production levels dropped and understaffed when they rose, but never perfectly balanced with the right number of employees.

When production decreased, management had to decide whether to let go of employees or carry the fixed cost. A few industries could afford to keep workers when business conditions did not justify doing so, but most companies had to let them go, a step they were very reluctant to take. Not only did layoffs increase their unemployment insurance taxes, but they also tarnished their reputation as an employer, consequently affecting their ability to recruit the best talent in the future. Furthermore, layoffs opened an employee wound for which unions provided emotional salve.

Figure 1. Patriarchal Workforce Model

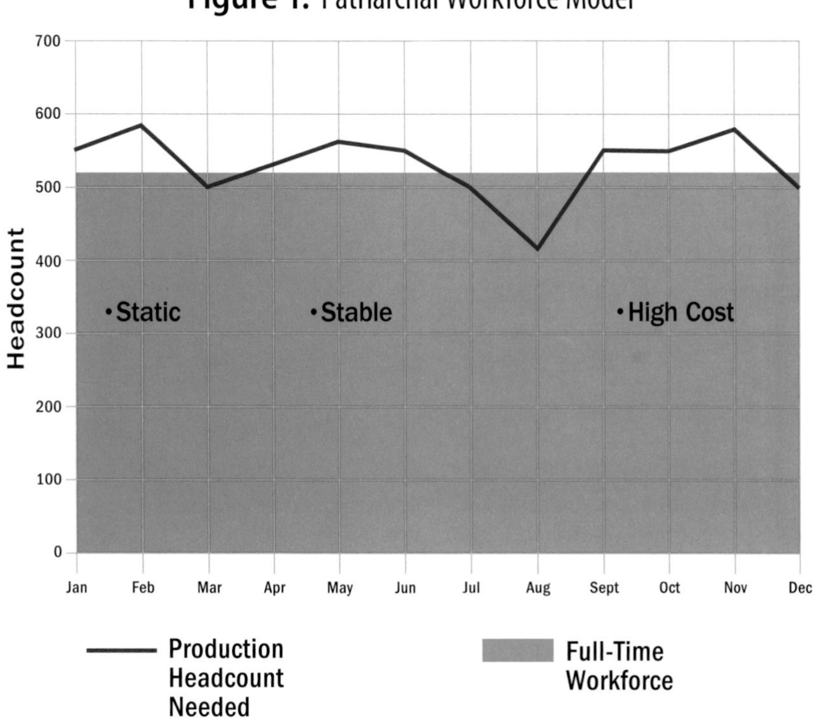

Workforce	Headcount											
	Jan	Feb	Mar	Apr	May	June	July	Aug	Sept	Oct	Nov	Dec
Full-Time	520	520	520	520	520	520	520	520	520	520	520	520
Production	**550**	**580**	**500**	**530**	**560**	**550**	**500**	**425**	**550**	**550**	**580**	**500**
Δ	-30	-60	+20	-10	-40	-30	+20	+95	-30	-30	-60	+20

On the other hand, when production ramped up faster than expected, organizations had to hire new personnel or work overtime. But hiring put pressure on the company to recruit, interview, select, and train totally new people—a long, expensive process to undertake to meet an immediate, unpredictable need. And working overtime not only increased the cost of the product but also led to decreased efficiency as employees put in longer hours.

So the Patriarchal Workforce Model saddled employers with having to make ongoing difficult decisions on over- and understaffing. In hindsight, we can see that this premium-priced family workforce offered very limited business flexibility and led to an ever-growing debt that was too far off to see but was real nonetheless. Today, such debts have come to be known as employee legacy costs.

Takeaways

- According to the first labor blueprint, the Patriarchal Workforce Model, people assumed that they'd be working for one company their entire lives.
- Huge corporate profits masked the escalating compensation and benefit costs that were generating a long-term employee legacy debt.
- Having only a static labor force at their disposal, employers had no effective staffing solutions for marketplace expansions and contractions.

FOUR

The 1970s Bring Flexibility

During WWII, millions of men left their jobs to serve their country, creating huge gaps in the workplace that had to be filled. This labor shortage planted the seeds of what we today refer to as the temporary staffing industry, which responds to businesses needing workers. By the 1970s, most large corporations had a growing dependency on such help for special projects and seasonal peaks, often utilizing twenty, fifty, one hundred, or even thousands of people.

This approach, known today as the **Staffing Workforce Model**, turned out to be a good one (see figure 2 on page 15). Companies could strategically balance labor needs and production levels by bringing in workers when they needed them and then letting them go when they did not—something they couldn't easily do with their own full-time employees. Organizations could now convert a historically fixed labor cost to a variable one while shifting liabilities for unemployment, EEOC matters, benefits, and worker's compensation to a third party.

Along with the practice of using temporary help came the increased reliance on contracted services to manage the low-skilled tasks, like cutting the grass, serving the food, cleaning the toilets, and guarding the front door. Although there was some internal political push back against eliminating these historically full-time jobs, everyone agreed that outside suppliers could provide these services cheaper and better.

Staffing Workforce Model:

Full-time employees combined with a flexible workforce consisting of temporary and contract workers, co-ops, and interns

At the same time, colleges and universities were offering another flexible workforce solution: co-ops. These programs allowed larger companies to rotate students through their organizations, sometimes for several years, and provide work experience for them. In many cases, this group of students became the future hiring pool. Co-op programs provided some variability in staffing, but for the most part, they were unmeasured, loosely administered, and wasteful.

Global businesses turned to yet another workforce option: internships. Organizations frequently sent young prodigies from the homeland to one of their locations in another country to represent corporate interests while providing that future star a taste of international business. But like their approach with co-ops, most companies failed to develop a methodology for measuring internships to identify the true return on investment.

Figure 2. Staffing Workforce Model

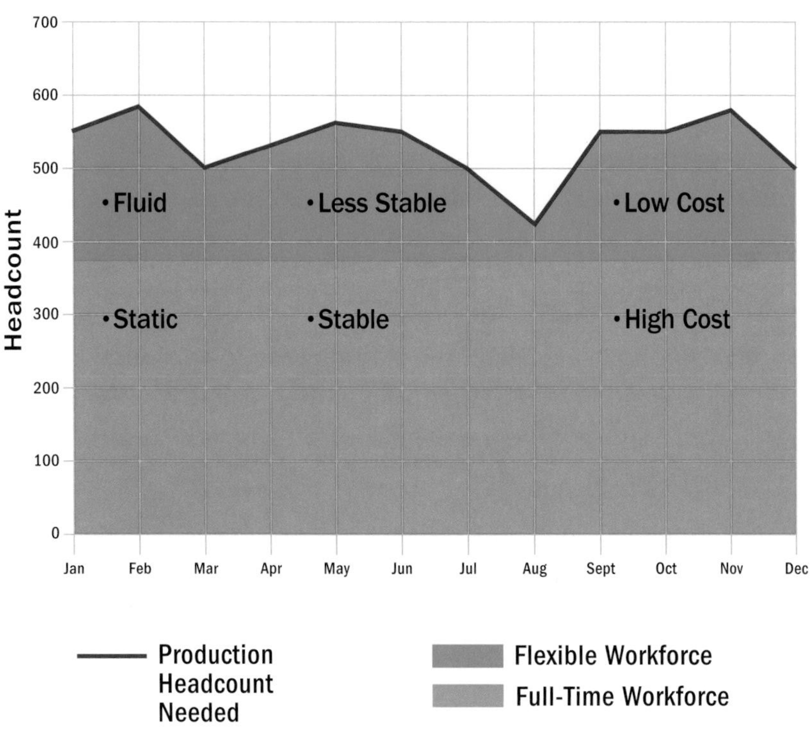

Workforce	Headcount											
	Jan	Feb	Mar	Apr	May	June	July	Aug	Sept	Oct	Nov	Dec
Flexible*	175	205	125	155	185	175	125	50	175	175	205	125
Full-Time	375	375	375	375	375	375	375	375	375	375	375	375
Total	550	580	500	530	560	550	500	425	550	550	580	500
Production	**550**	**580**	**500**	**530**	**560**	**550**	**500**	**425**	**550**	**550**	**580**	**500**

*Temporary and contract workers, co-ops, and interns.

Tremendously helpful, the Staffing Workforce Model introduced business leaders to the concept of using outside contractors and services to better manage their companies and respond to changing market conditions.

Takeaways

- The seeds of the temporary workforce were planted during WWII.
- Maturing in the 1970s, the Staffing Workforce Model combined full-time employees with a flexible workforce consisting of temporary and contract workers, co-ops, and interns.
- Companies could now balance labor and production levels while converting some of the fixed labor costs to variable ones and mitigating employee liabilities.

FIVE

Hidden Costs of Temp Workers

During the early days of temporary staffing in the 1960s and '70s, most companies turned to this option on a short-term, project, or seasonal basis only. As they started to increase their number of temporary workers, the enormous cost savings caught the attention of the number crunchers. Before long, some "temporary" jobs were lasting two, three, or five years, and others would end only if the business folded.

Organizations began viewing this labor expense as a commodity, listing it as a line item on the corporate profit and loss statement. Subsequently, the responsibility for it shifted from HR to the purchasing department with two goals in mind: obtain the lowest price and the most extended payment terms.

Companies could now finance what originally was a statutory, fixed payroll cost as a variable one. Instead of having to accommodate government-mandated payroll timetables for their full-time employees, a business could stretch out that payment to a temporary-staffing vendor for thirty, sixty, ninety, or more days.

Some of the savings in using temporary workers were staggering. The fully loaded bill rate of a staffing provider was often one-half—sometimes even one-quarter—of the company's full-time pay rate alone, and the savings in benefit and statutory costs were typically 30–45 percent on top of that. So it's easy to understand why the number of temporary workers continued to swell and why businesses increased this group as a percentage of their overall labor force.

Eventually, companies sought to leverage this expense even further by bundling regional, nationwide, and global staffing contracts. Typically, the firm offering the cheapest hourly bill rate won the business. Because 80 percent of every hourly bill rate for temporary services was (and still is) directly related to the employee's wage, higher pay rates translated into higher bill rates, and lower pay rates translated into lower bill rates. Companies wanted the cheapest bill rate, so temporary-worker wages were steadily suppressed over time. Number crunchers squeezed all they could out of the Staffing Model, even beating down competing staffing suppliers to the final pennies that separated their respective hourly bill rates.

This practice of applying cookie-cutter, commodity pricing to people comes at a huge cost. As the temporary staffing industry matured, the typically large disparity in pay between full-time regular employees and temps gave rise to a wide gap in the quality and dedication levels between the two types of workers. Let's face it: if you're making half the wage of the person sitting next to you who is performing the same job, will you have the same degree of commitment?

Out of this scenario emerged a two-class employee system. Class one consisted of well-trained, full-time, and stable employees who enjoyed market-based pay and competitive benefits. Tenure and loyalty in this group were strong.

On the other hand, members of class two—the temporary class—had quite the opposite experience. Their wages were as low as procurement could negotiate them, and their benefits were likewise few, if any. So, as you would expect, when compared to class one, this group exhibited much different characteristics in the workplace:

- Lower morale
- Higher absenteeism
- Greater turnover
- Less efficiency
- Poorer work quality

Well-meaning purchasing and finance departments were tasked with saving money on what companies paid for the hourly bill rate, but they didn't realize that their businesses were becoming less efficient. More labor hours were required to get the same amount of work done, largely due to exorbitant turnover and absenteeism, as well as constant retraining. It was not unusual for temporary annual turnover to average 200–400 percent on large staffing projects and for absenteeism to reach as high as 35 percent. Could you run a company like that?

Because temporary workers affected the quality and efficiency of operations, their true cost went far beyond the hourly bill rate. Although the number crunchers saved a few cents per hour negotiating that rate, production was absorbing 10–20 percent more in labor hours for completing the same amount of work. They were unknowingly penny wise and dollar foolish.

The impact of these liabilities on quality, delivery, and waste was the hardest to measure. Because no one was factoring these variables into the hourly bill rate, companies had no clue what it was really costing them to use a temporary workforce.

At this time, businesses began adopting another often-misaligned staffing approach: the Temp-to-Perm Hiring Model.

Temp-to-Perm Hiring Model:

A full-time workforce drawn almost exclusively from a pool of low-paid temporary workers

To illustrate, let's say for a particular job, temporary workers were paid $7 an hour and their full-time counterparts were paid $14. When a position opened up, the easiest way to fill it was to grab John or Mary "Temp"—someone with a proven track record—and plug him or her in at $14 an hour.

Before this practice took hold, the same company would have placed an ad in the newspaper. Instead, hiring managers made their selection from the temporary workforce, paying a $7-an-hour worker $14 an hour when they could have hired the same person for possibly half that amount. What caliber of worker could they have gotten for $14 an hour had they gone into the marketplace? By taking the easy route, they inadvertently weakened the quality of their workforce.

Those organizations still using this model exacerbate the problem when they fail to set their full-time hourly pay rates to a true market valuation. If the job in the above example is actually valued at $10 an hour, but you're paying the full-time employee $14 and the temporary worker is earning $7, you have a problem. You're substantially overpaying your full-time employees (who are by now far less efficient than they were during their first year of employment), and at the same time, you aren't paying enough to attract the highest-quality temporary workers.

If you continue to hire from your temporary pool, you must be willing to pay more and move closer to the job's fair market value. If you choose not to do so, in the long term, you will dramatically reduce your competitive edge derived through your workers.

Takeaways

- While companies have realized tremendous cost savings by utilizing a temporary workforce, they have unknowingly forfeited many of those savings in wasteful, unmeasured ways.
- Over time, the compensation and benefit gap between temporary and full-time workers has widened.
- You must determine a current market valuation of wages and benefit scales for both temporary and full-time workers, especially if you hire from the temporary group.

SIX

Paying the Piper

In the twenty-first century, as the global marketplace has continued to expand, executives have felt increasing competitive pressure to improve their financial performance. The employee legacy costs we discussed in chapter 3 are finally coming home to roost and things have gotten ugly. Some of the Family members are feeling like redheaded stepchildren as they lose benefits, job security, and—in many cases—their actual job. Indeed, in desperation, companies have reacted with solutions like these:

- Slashed retiree benefits
- Reduced wages
- Cut-to-the-bone layoffs
- Pensions replaced by 401(k)s
- Employee buyouts
- Involuntary separations

Perhaps the biggest change has come in the area of health care benefits—and more changes are on the way in 2014. What typically started with co-pays and higher deductibles has deteriorated into no medical insurance at all.

Without a doubt, executives and business owners will—and must—continue to inflict tremendous pain on their full-time employees for some time to come. I call this period the "great legacy unraveling."

What has happened to cause these Family-friendly, too-big-to-fail corporations to take such drastic steps?

- New global competitors have less expensive, more efficient labor and business models.
- Western businesses have allowed the cost of many jobs—hourly, exempt, and nonexempt—to exceed their bottom-line value. They are paying too much!
- Maybe most importantly, although companies are correctly attacking costs in relentless fashion, they still focus too much time on nonessential business functions and processes.

To its credit, the Staffing Workforce Model addresses some of these business issues. As figure 2 on page 15 indicates, organizations can operate with a fluid, low-cost—yet less stable—flexible workforce while still maintaining a static, stable—yet high-cost—full-time one. This is a good approach but offers only a partial solution.

Now don't get me wrong: I believe in the temporary help industry. In fact, MAU is one of the largest independent providers of such help. But we're especially eager to work with customers who will talk with us strategically. Once we understand a company's goals, business model, and specific functions and processes, we can discuss the different types of workforces that would be most cost-effective, efficient, and qualitatively sound.

Unfortunately, up to this point, too many business leaders haven't experienced enough discomfort to make them look inward and implement such long-term, strategic workforce changes. As we emerge from the current recession, I believe that now might just be the time.

Takeaways

- Employee legacy costs, once a speck on the distant horizon, have grown proportionally too large for today's businesses to ignore.
- By failing to look at their workforces strategically, companies have become less competitive in the global marketplace.
- Although the Patriarchal and Staffing models were once effective, their incomplete designs, combined with the economic crisis, are insufficient alone to address the complex needs of twenty-first-century businesses.

SEVEN

A New Business Blueprint

Recently, I talked with a friend of mine who is an executive with a successful Tier 1 international automotive supplier. At each of the eight plants he oversees, the normal business model is in place: manufacturing, finance, engineering, IT, administration, purchasing, quality, logistics, and HR. Actually, one of the functions I mentioned above—manufacturing—is a misnomer. You see, although his company does manufacture automotive products, each of his plants is only responsible for assembling them. In other words, the product is made elsewhere and then shipped to each of the plants for final assembly and just-in-time delivery to an OEM.

I told my friend about my frustration with executives who were reluctant to take a fresh look at their businesses and get to their real core. Why didn't they spend more time identifying and focusing on those activities that would differentiate their companies and make them more competitive?

I went on to say, "Frank, you're responsible for a number of plants across North America, and they're doing a great job of assembling products for your customers. But in my opinion, all your facilities do nothing but noncore work. The incredible overhead you've maintained all these years adds no value to your product—they are assembly plants, for crying out loud." He responded, "I suppose what you're saying is true, Randy. Maybe we just keep reading the same old business blueprint we've been using for years, assuming that it's the right thing to do."

Executives don't question their own business models for a variety of reasons. They might be unaware of other options or worried that if sweeping change occurred, their position would be affected. What if their whole division or department were outsourced to a third-party specialist?

I've decided, though, that most leaders don't engage in new strategic thinking because they're just too busy to squeeze in another project, especially one that would necessitate overcoming the tremendous inertia of their company's old blueprint.

Takeaways

- It sometimes takes an outside perspective to jolt executives into shifting away from a dated, inefficient model and toward a lean one centered on value-added core activities.
- For a number of companies, doing the same thing year after year—despite a steady decline in the marketplace—is better than risking the unknown.
- Many leaders continue to follow their old business blueprint because their packed schedules don't afford them the time to design a new one.

EIGHT

Start Your Journey

A successful blueprint for companies competing in today's global economy takes a strategic approach to the workforce and seeks to reduce or eliminate the crippling long-term employee legacy costs. According to this model, leaders focus all their time, resources, and creative efforts on their core activities by outsourcing their noncore activities to third parties that focus on them as *their* core.

Your Greatest Value

To tailor such a model to your particular needs, you must first identify and classify all the areas in your organization. Begin the process by walking the floors of your company and jotting down the different jobs, departments, and functions represented there. To aid in this exercise, visit http://www.mau.com/resources for a downloadable, interactive form you can use to quickly list what you observe (see figure 3 on page 28). I recommend evaluating one department at a time to make this initial step easier on your schedule.

Figure 3. Core/Noncore Walk-Through

Job Title/Function	Core	Noncore	
		Critical	Noncritical

When you've completed your plant tour, move down your list and mark off your core business functions by answering the following questions:

- Which activities add unique value to your product or service and thereby differentiate you from your competitors?
- What are you known for?
- What are your customers willing to pay you for?

- If you had only one company dollar to spend in the next five years, which activities would you invest in to become more competitive?

To illustrate, I recently directed the last question to a group of senior manufacturing executives. I discovered that although their products differed, the manufacturers agreed on what they had to concentrate on to be more competitive. They chose four areas of investment:

1. Equipment and automation
2. Sales and marketing
3. Mergers and acquisitions
4. R&D and innovation

These executives also shared sound thinking. Regarding equipment and automation, manufacturers in particular must continue to become more efficient, so they should focus their efforts on this area. As far as sales and marketing are concerned, I believe that they are saying they have to get closer to their customers—closer to what they want and require—and be totally in tune with them. Mergers and acquisitions relate to the manufacturers' requirement to increase their capital resources so they can merge with and acquire competitors, and expand into new business segments. Finally, R&D and innovation are crucial because manufacturers know that they have to get to the market first with new and better products, and deliver tomorrow what today is unimaginable.

As you answer the questions above, turn to your colleagues for their feedback and insights, and fine-tune your list. I've found

that when executives finish identifying all their core functions for the first time, they are often amazed by the low total. In fact, at an average manufacturing facility, as few as 50 percent of the jobs and processes might belong in this category.

Everything Else

The remaining activities on your walk-through list are probably noncore and fall into one of two subcategories: critical or noncritical. For purposes of definition going forward, the latter will refer to activities that have little to do with the business itself but are necessary in some way, like the janitorial, security, food service, and lawn-keeping tasks I mentioned in chapter 4. The reality is that every company on the block has these types of needs.

The "critical" subcategory contains the remaining noncore jobs, those still handled in most cases by full-time employees, such as HR, payroll, accounting, IT, and maintenance.

Figure 4. Core/Noncore Analysis

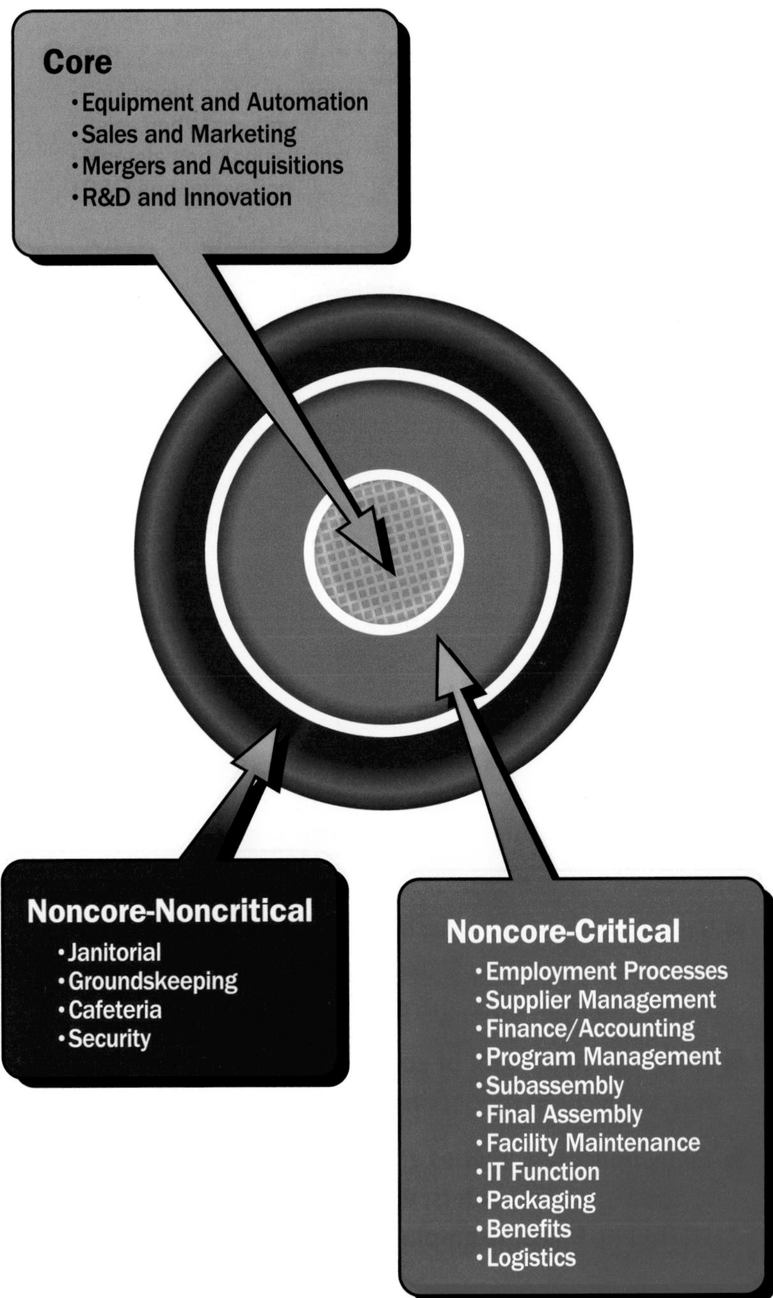

Most of the items in both noncore columns are fair game for management by third parties that focus on them as their core. The upshot is they can usually offer better, faster, and often cheaper options!

Although not conclusive, figure 4 provides other examples of what pertains to each of the three descriptive areas. Beyond the low-hanging fruit of noncore-noncritical outsourcing, turn your thinking toward noncore-critical business activities. The possibilities for outsourcing these are as varied as the different types of companies and products sold. MAU has managed functions ranging from the simple to the complex: logistics, subassembly, final assembly, fulfillment centers, employment, raw material movement, and robotic cells.

As you'll see, this area provides the best opportunities for stretching your mind—and securing a stronghold in the marketplace.

Takeaways

- Take a hands-on approach to determining your core and noncore business by walking the floors of your plant and reviewing each function, process, and activity yourself.
- As few as 50 percent of your current jobs, processes, and functions could be classified as core.
- Many noncore activities are candidates for outsourcing to third-party providers, even though they are currently staffed by full-time employees.

NINE

If Time Is Money

How do you spend your time? We have only so many hours a day in which to accomplish our goals. What we think about and act on every day directly affects the short- and long-term outcomes of our businesses and careers.

Take, for example, an experience our company has had with a nonunion consumer products manufacturer with which we have worked side by side for over thirty years. Together, we have journeyed through almost all the changes and evolutions referenced in the previous chapters.

Historically, like many other nonunion manufacturers, our customer provided compensation and benefits that were influenced by union scales. Consequently, they were plagued with high employee costs for noncore jobs, resulting in labor expenditures far above market-based averages. This issue became more problematic as these expenses exceeded those of some of their newer rivals. How quickly could they erase the double-time, triple-time, and exorbitant salaries, along with benefit packages, that enabled a material handler in the 1980s to earn $80,000 a year and an unskilled worker to earn $55,000?

We worked together to identify their noncore-critical functions, and ultimately our company assumed responsibility for managing many of them. In retrospect, we provided our customer with an unforeseen benefit equal to or greater than the cost savings and efficiencies: we brought them focus. Their managers had more hours in the day to concentrate on the parts of the business that would make them more productive and profitable.

This customer continued to push the envelope by turning more and more noncore-critical functions over to our company. Several years later, a top executive there told me that he had to rely on us to perform with excellence so he and his team could continue focusing on their core processes every day. In other words, he said, "We make paper, and I need to spend all my energy thinking about how we can make a higher-quality product both faster and cheaper. I can't afford to be distracted by other areas. I need your company to take care of them."

He went on to say he realized that he had just so much time in a day and that the things he thought about would be those he improved upon. He didn't want to figure out how to improve the way they packaged, wrapped, sorted, or shipped his product, because he knew that other companies could handle those functions better than his could. Being able to outpace his competitors largely depended on innovation in product design and leveraged production capabilities. That was his new *focus!*

It is intriguing to me how companies come to their awakening, their moment of enlightenment—that point in time when they have perfect clarity about their mission, their reason for being in business, and their uniqueness. Years later, this same executive was pressed in an open business forum to explain how his company had identified which jobs, processes, and functions were most critical. He could not have spoken more poignant words when he replied, "It's those jobs that *touch* the paper." How about that for clarity and focus?

At the same forum, the friend I mentioned in the introduction who waited anxiously for the Friday conference calls was asked the same question. He gave a similar answer: "It is those jobs that *touch* the metal." Today, not only is his aluminum-smelting plant a survivor in the company system and industry, but it remains a low-cost, top-quality, and high-efficiency leader. How have he and his team achieved this distinction? In good part, their success comes from continuing to pinpoint which core jobs and processes they should manage and invest in.

Thus, if you work in these two international companies and don't "touch the paper" or "touch the metal," then your job will likely be managed by a third party. The logic for doing so is simple: free up the company's talent and resources to concentrate on how to become more competitive.

Am I getting any clearer now? What is it that makes your business unique? Imagine if you had more time to focus on your uniqueness every day. What if by outsourcing all your noncore responsibilities, you could gain that freedom? What better investment can you make to ensure you stay ahead of your rivals?

In the chapters ahead, I would like to direct your attention toward specific noncore-critical activities that I believe most companies have not yet explored: the employment function, financial responsibilities, program management, and facility maintenance. In most organizations, outsourcing these areas will affect existing full-time jobs, and in some organizations, that translates into stepping on sacred cows. Yet outsourcing is exactly what you need to do to improve your company's performance and take the lead in your industry.

How Do You Spend Your Time?

Takeaways

- What you think about and act on every day affects the short- and long-term outcomes of your business and career.
- Those companies that clearly differentiate between their core functions and those they can turn over to third parties will realize a competitive advantage.
- Business leaders must be willing to make difficult decisions, which can include terminating full-time employees—even those at the top.

TEN

HR's New Best Friend

What could be more important than your role as gatekeeper of the culture and soul of your company? Determining how to attract and hire the finest talent is one of the most critical business decisions you'll ever make. And yet regardless of the hiring process you adopt, its greatest value to your company occurs only during the final interviewing phase, when you and your team can look candidates square in the eye and ultimately decide whether they are the right fit for your company. The rest of the process is simply a means to an end.

For that reason, the employment function lends itself perfectly to outsourcing. This front-office activity is not unique to any industry, and there are experts who possess greater skills, systems, and efficiencies than any person or department within your organization. Why? Because that's all they do every day, 24/7. They ought to perform this task better, faster, and maybe even cheaper than your company can.

Staffing and recruiting organizations exist to find temporary, contract, and full-time talent. Just as you are dedicated to making your product and delivering your service, they are dedicated to bringing you the right people at the right time and at the right price.

With just one phone call, MAU can recruit hundreds of new workers for your company while you focus on your core business. Recently, one of my board members shook his head in disbelief when I presented a graph indicating we had hired 700 employees for a customer within a two-month period. He remarked that when his company had to hire only seventy people, it was enough to create incredible stress and disruption throughout the entire organization.

The Employment Function:

Any activity that touches the internal or external movement of labor to accommodate changing business demands

Many companies today are growing more familiar with Recruitment Process Outsourcing (RPO), whereby a third party assumes responsibility for all their external recruiting. This service becomes even more valuable when business leaders use it for outsourcing the entire employment function: bringing in new talent (external movement) as well as relocating workers within an organization (internal movement).

External Movement

An RPO solution for hiring external employees can give you a leg up on your competition by enabling you to reach the talent first so you can make the job offer first. The measurement tools offered through this lean and transparent system ensure integrity and efficiency in every step of the process.

Without such a solution in place, many companies fail to fulfill their responsibilities when they turn to a recruiting service. Looking for talent, they'll call on such a business, which works quickly to send them qualified resumes, but then they might take a week or longer to provide feedback. In that time, the candidates have other interviews and receive job offers, and the process must start all over.

> **External Movement:**
>
> The acquisition of outside talent that will fit in one or more of these job categories: full-time regular, part-time, intern, co-op, contractor, temporary, or outsourced

Companies often demand full accountability on the recruiter's part but don't place the same expectations on their organization, unknowingly paying the price in long-term vacancies and higher recruiting costs. However, when the processes they are accountable for are held to a standard or KPI (Key Performance Indicators), companies can improve their access to the best talent available—while lowering their hiring expenses.

In a lean RPO system, every step is measured, process takt times are set, and accountability and escalation plans are established for all parties involved. Everyone can view this real-time data on the Internet and stay informed.

In a well-established RPO, MAU will submit a short list of qualified candidates for professional positions to the customer in as little as three days. From there, if everyone stays in compliance, a new employee could be starting in under six weeks—

Figure 5. External Recruiting Process Outsourcing
Sales & Marketing

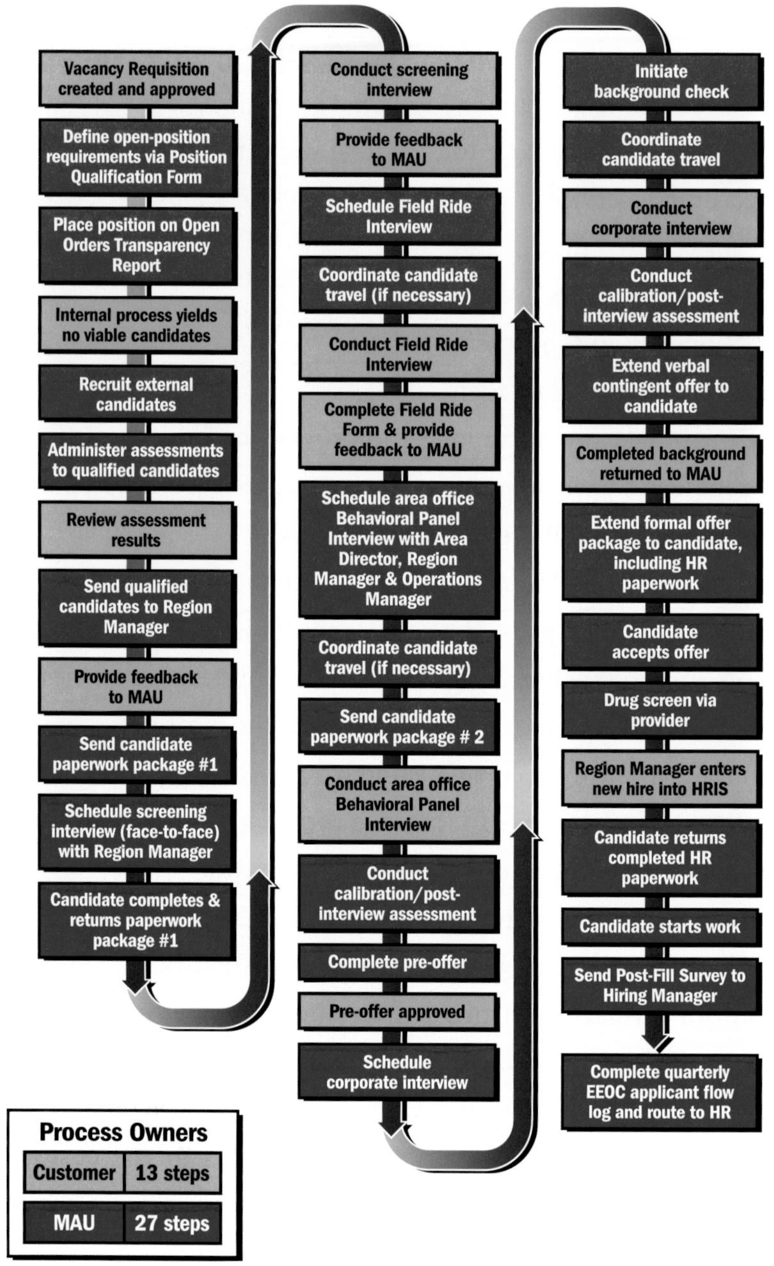

and that includes the two-week notice period. See figure 5 for the typical steps performed during this process.

Here are the many advantages of transferring your external recruitment tasks to an RPO provider:

Economic

- Reduce your recruiting costs 15–40 percent
- Convert fixed costs to variable ones

Strategic

- Transform recruiting from a staff function to a strategic advantage
- Enhance the overall quality of talent and bench strength

Operational

- Obtain Service Level Agreements (SLAs) based on metrics and quantifiable results
- Improve throughput and enjoy higher satisfaction levels with standardized, world-class processes
- Save time with a single point of contact to manage all your staffing and recruiting service providers

Flexibility and Scalability

- Scale up and down as your business needs change

Human Resources

- Free HR to focus on strategic workforce planning and management

Technology

- Gain access to the best recruiting technology solutions

Risk Management

- Improve compliance

A Case in Point

An international Fortune 50 medical products organization with a sales force of 350 across North America turned to MAU for solutions. Their regional and district managers tended to use different recruiters, sometimes following the company's hiring processes and sometimes not. Vacancies remained unfilled for months, and the hiring team dropped too many balls when coordinating with the corporate office. Gross inefficiencies were costing the company top sales candidates and millions of dollars in lost sales opportunities.

As our solution, we developed and implemented a comprehensive recruiting and hiring process (RPO), making it completely transparent to corporate and regional leadership and standardizing it across the U.S. and Canadian sales teams. We instituted quality checks with short feedback cycles to expedite recruitment and selection, renegotiated and coordinated third-party recruiting-agency contracts, and managed all administrative duties.

Within six months, our customer saw improvements in every key area. Because MAU managed the most time-consuming functions, members of the sales force could reduce their involvement in the hiring process 70 percent—from forty-two steps to thirteen—freeing them to concentrate on core competencies: sales! Open positions were filled 42 percent faster and the candidate quality increased by 50 percent. This process proved so successful that our customer instituted RPO models globally in all its operations.

In partnership with another customer, we designed a current-state and future-state process flowchart as part of an external RPO. When we finished diagramming all the steps, we asked the HR team which ones they ascribed value to. One manager responded, "That's easy—when a new employee is sitting in the seat." Hmm. If that's the case, why are most companies still managing the entire hiring process themselves?

Co-ops and Internships

Two of the best sources of variable-cost, professional labor that can yield the highest long-term ROI are the co-op and internship models. On a domestic level, most employers have developed relationships with colleges, universities, and various educational entities to help them locate these resources. However, as mentioned in chapter 4, the costs to administer these programs are often buried in a departmental budget. In most companies, the HR department allocates some part of fixed headcount for annual road trips to schools, follow-up visits, PR, program management, and other related activities. International internships need separate management and resources, since visas, work permits, and housing could be required along with language accommodations.

Each time one co-op or intern is used for even a semester, as many as thirty administrative activities have to be completed. In addition to absorbing the fixed overhead to manage these programs, companies also carry the liability and other employer-related costs to keep the workers on their payroll.

The opportunity for savings exists when you can simply make a request to your outsourced partners for "x" number of interns or co-ops for a certain length of time. These partners bear the ongoing costs and deliverables for program design and management. They recruit, hire on to their payroll (not yours), and just give you what's valuable to your company: an individual sitting in the seat. The best part is that you benefit from an ROI model that finally evaluates your program costs and increases yields tied to bench-strength objectives.

Managed Service Providers

Although I don't expound on them in this book, I'd like to acknowledge the skyrocketing growth of Managed Service Providers (MSPs). Taking external RPO to the next level, these firms manage the staffing supply chain by using advanced technologies to maximize efficiencies and cost savings. They typically focus on order distribution, billing, and performance.

To optimize the supplier base, MSPs ensure that vendors conform to standardized processes, as well as to terms and pricing schedules across the customer's entire platform of locations, job disciplines, and business segments. On average, companies that contract with these providers can expect to save in the neighborhood of 10-15 percent of the total staffing expense.

MSPs are capable of offering their services while also being one of the preferred vendors in the supply chain. In many cases, though, they remain vendor neutral, simply managing staffing-related contracts across a company's platform without providing any staffing services themselves.

Internal Movement

So far, I have focused on savings and efficiencies that can be realized through RPO solutions for external recruitment. You can experience comparable benefits by outsourcing your internal employment process in the same manner.

The movement of existing employees falls within the following broad categories:

- Job to job
- Shift to shift
- Plant (location) to plant (location)
- Country to country
- Continent to continent

For both hourly and salaried employees, large employers use some type of job-bidding or posting system that typically includes many steps and moving parts: scheduling interviews, verifying skills and experience, ranking candidates, obtaining sign-offs and signatures, communicating rejections, coordinating with payroll, and so forth. At most sizable organizations, every time an employee bids or otherwise applies for an internal job opening, a minimum of eleven processes have to be completed for each person, and an additional eight processes for the employee who subsequently moves. To verify these numbers, look carefully at all the steps involved in your company's approach and make your own process flow.

> **Internal Movement:**
> The relocation of employees within an organization that occurs primarily through promotions and transfers

Simply put, organizations must accommodate a great deal of activity and costs to promote or transfer employees. Although the management of this process is important, I would like to point out that no part adds value to a company's product or service offering, making this hybrid RPO model such a worthwhile option.

Takeaways

- Growing in popularity, Recruitment Process Outsourcing (RPO) can help HR departments reduce hiring costs while improving efficiency.
- To obtain the most value from RPO, companies need to consider using it for both internal and external workforce movement.
- Co-op and internship initiatives can be significantly enhanced through programs managed by third parties.

ELEVEN

The Company Rudder

Finance and Accounting Outsourcing (FAO) is increasingly gaining favor among controllers, CFOs, and other C-level executives. Maturing significantly over the last decade, this alternative approach to managing internal accounting operations can satisfy a wide range of financial needs. What historically began as a play for labor arbitrage–based costs savings has developed into a full-service industry, whose providers essentially occupy a strategic seat at the corporate table.

Not only do FAO partners offer transaction-based "vanilla" services, such as accounts payable and accounts receivable, but they also handle the more complex, decision-based functions, such as management reporting, analytics, and risk management. Many companies choose to carve out just a specific set of functions to outsource, whereas others transition almost all their finance and accounting processes, barring strategic debt financing and support of enterprise strategies (fig. 6).

Figure 6. Finance & Accounting Outsourcing

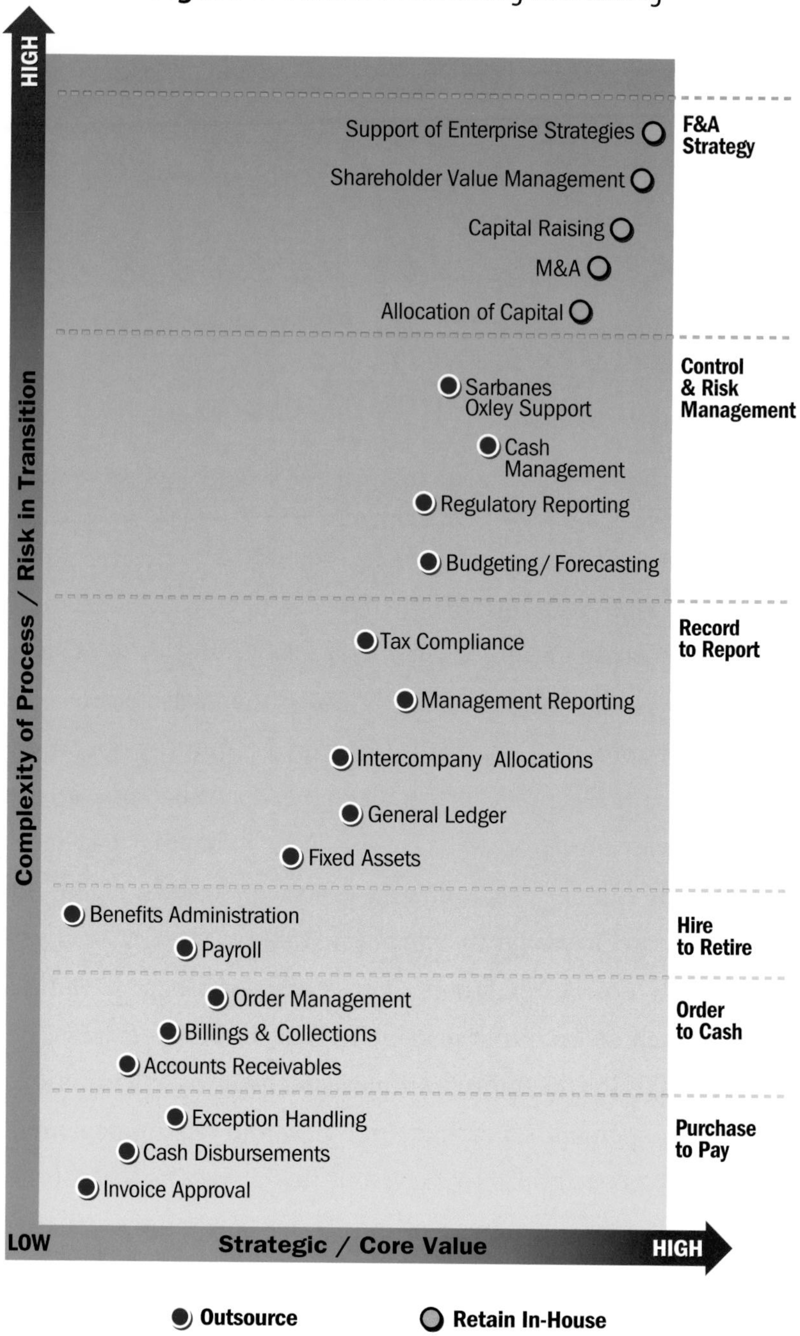

HIGH

Complexity of Process / Risk in Transition

F&A Strategy

Support of Enterprise Strategies
Shareholder Value Management
Capital Raising
M&A
Allocation of Capital

Control & Risk Management

Sarbanes Oxley Support
Cash Management
Regulatory Reporting
Budgeting / Forecasting

Record to Report

Tax Compliance
Management Reporting
Intercompany Allocations
General Ledger
Fixed Assets

Hire to Retire

Benefits Administration
Payroll

Order to Cash

Order Management
Billings & Collections
Accounts Receivables

Purchase to Pay

Exception Handling
Cash Disbursements
Invoice Approval

LOW Strategic / Core Value HIGH

● Outsource ○ Retain In-House

The level of confidence entrusted in FAO has grown in part from the maturing capabilities of the service providers, which have developed tried-and-true methodologies for transferring processes seamlessly—without interruption or exception. These partners offer well-structured governance frameworks that effectively manage risk and align outsourcing with the larger objectives of the business. Further, they guarantee service levels and build measurement tools to monitor metrics and ensure ongoing process health, focusing their efforts on continuous improvement and process engineering.

While FAO has streamlined operations and improved the speed and availability of information, an even greater benefit is the amount of time it gives the leadership to focus on strategic, value-added activities. The responsibilities of today's CFOs and finance departments reach beyond the traditional functions of cash applications, reconciliations, closing the books, and management reporting. Although these tasks have not disappeared, the finance team is expected to shoulder strategic-level ones as well. Working to eliminate the siloed internal departments of the past, many companies are choosing to integrate financial functions throughout their organizations to take better advantage of real-time market performance.

In fact, senior executives are now positioning the finance department as the company "rudder," relying on it to furnish data and analysis that will improve decision-making. In addition to providing the day-to-day operational intelligence to the field, the finance team must meet the challenges of new and ever-changing regulatory requirements, business growth, market demand, and global expansion. Consequently, the finance staff has been saddled with increasingly arduous responsibilities—many of which are strategic in nature.

By transferring the daily tasks of maintaining the books and records to a third party, companies can forgo the regular duties related to recruiting, training, and employee management. Organizations can now access a ready supply of highly skilled, specialized talent—often CPAs, global Chartered Accountants, and MBAs—who are up to date on regulatory topics and experienced across a range of industries.

This model essentially converts the business's cost structure from fixed to variable and allows executives to more easily ramp employees up and down with business cycles. No matter whether companies select a provider located onshore, nearshore, or offshore, they will enjoy significant cost savings in the form of labor arbitrage and more efficient processing.

Typical benefits of FAO include the following:

- Cost savings of 30–60 percent from offshore outsourcing and ongoing process improvement
- Access to hard-to-find skill sets and specialized talent—including CPAs, Chartered Accountants, and MBAs
- A flexible workforce structure, with the ability to quickly expand or pare back operations
- Ongoing focus on improving process efficiency and effectiveness
- Expertise in finance and accounting best practices, functional benchmarks, and process engineering
- Experience integrating and implementing add-on, nondisruptive, and enabling technologies
- High-quality service based on SLAs and process metrics

- Concentrated efforts in risk management and regulatory compliance
- Proven transition methodologies and governance frameworks

According to Vince Sparrow, Senior Managing Director of Outsourced Partners International, "FAO has emerged as a facilitator for companies seeking to reinvent the role and function of their finance team. By turning to a third party—for either a supplement to or a full replacement of in-house operations—executives are finding it easier to implement change throughout their organizations and develop agile, optimized business models."

Few business applications offer a better opportunity to take advantage of expert professional and technological resources that can be integrated at a very manageable, logical pace. When you decide to invest in this process, you will be quickly rewarded as you encounter world-class providers with smart business solutions.

Takeaways

- Because CFO responsibilities are expanding in complexity and scope, business leaders must be prudent in managing all resources and expenses.
- By partnering with a Finance and Accounting Outsourcing (FAO) service provider, companies can augment their finance team with global employees trained in customized processes and contractually dedicated to delivering quality services.
- Companies can now transfer day-to-day tasks to a third party at a fraction of the historical cost, giving CFOs the freedom to focus on strategic activities that support the growing business.

TWELVE

Another Tool for Your Toolbox

Chances are you've taken part in business team exercises that challenge you to think differently. Perhaps like me, you've felt uncomfortable having your fears and doubts exposed in such situations. For instance, would you consider letting a partner manage a pilot program for you? How should you ramp up new products while balancing production of the older ones? Are you still carrying 4 to 8 percent in fixed annual headcount costs just to accommodate employee absenteeism?

Like many business leaders, you would probably respond to these program management questions the same way you did twenty years ago. Do something radical instead. Turn to experienced, third-party specialists for timely, creative solutions.

Pilot Programs

New products and models come and go at a faster pace than ever as consumers insist on the latest and greatest service and features. The market will continue to demand more and more choices, faster and faster. Strategic outsourcing offers a method for managing new pilot programs without disrupting existing operations and obligating the company to long-term, fixed costs.

For instance, in the late 1990s, an international OEM approached us about launching a test program for a new vehicle that, if successful, would be integrated into one of their plants. Manufactured in China, the parts would be shipped to Charleston, South Carolina, and then brought to a Georgia-based assembly facility, where they would subsequently be assembled and distributed to dealers across North America.

As part of our partnership, we secured an off-site facility near one of our customer's existing plants and managed an actual final assembly line owned by them. MAU hired a team of thirty-five employees who would ultimately bear full responsibility for importing the unassembled vehicle, coordinating transportation to the assembly facility, assembling the vehicle, and distributing it to the dealer network. See figure 7 on page 54.

To evaluate the new vehicle, our customer scheduled a one-year pilot program. But one year wasn't long enough so they asked us for a second year and then a third. After three years, the vehicle was deemed a success, and then—and only then—did they turn this assembly responsibility over to one of their existing plants with fixed costs. Management made a smart decision, considering this vehicle is one of their most profitable models today.

Ramp-Up and Ramp-Down Programs

The shelf life of most merchandise is shortening. Because consumers expect the latest and greatest technology, functionality,

Figure 7. Kit Assembly Process

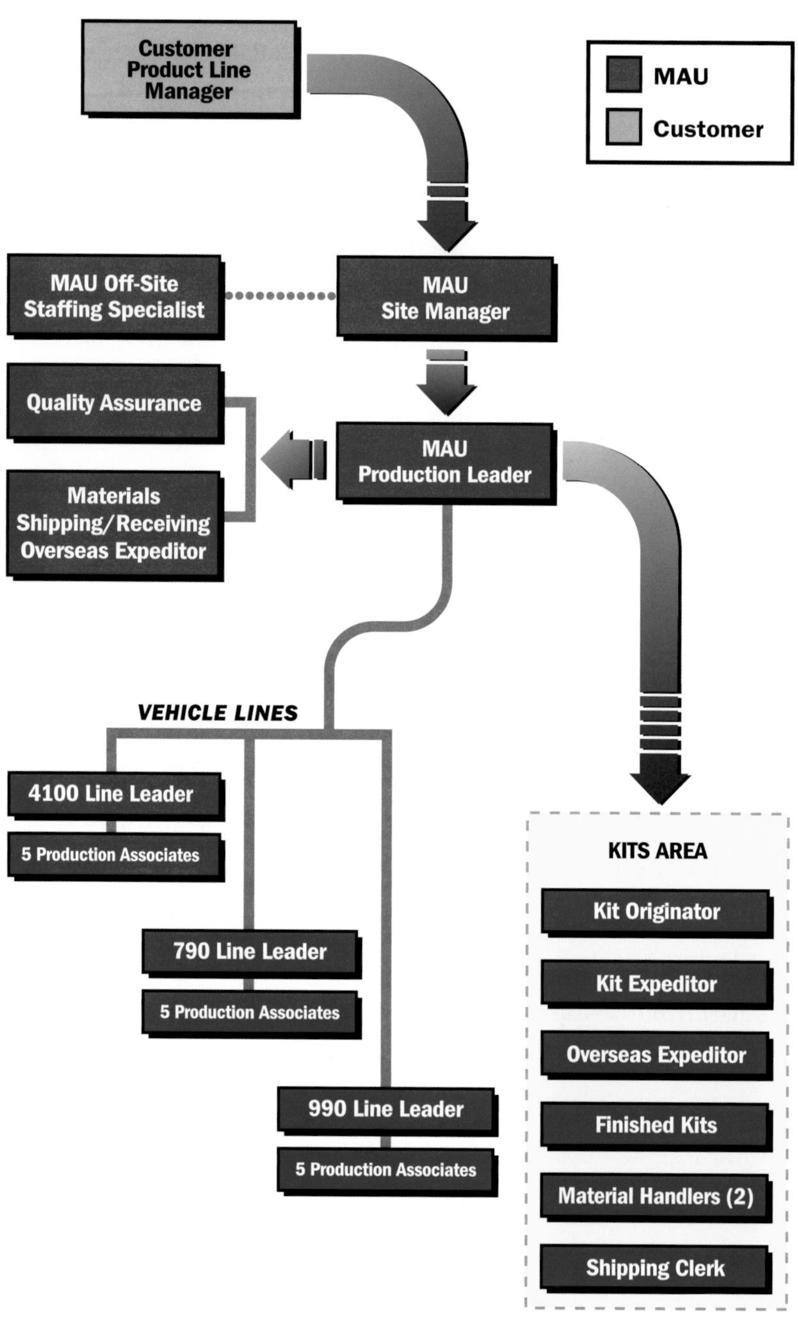

and quality, companies are speeding up the cycle time between new and old products and versions. Where will the additional labor come from for your next ramp-up or offering? Of course, you could hire new employees, but once the older model has ramped down, you would be overstaffed. So you must choose between laying off employees or carrying a fixed headcount for what could be an indefinite period. Needless to say, neither option is desirable.

An alternative lies in developing a partnership with a strategic workforce designer that fully understands your business and knows how to move labor in, around, and out of your organization.

At our company, we have found that most manufacturing and high-touch assembly operations have a handful—a small percentage—of core positions and the rest can be best managed by a third party. Figure 8 on page 56 shows a final assembly line of a Tier 1 automotive supplier. For a particular product, our customer was phasing out the oldest model while preparing for the newest one slated for production within six months. To facilitate the ramp-down, MAU would provide an outsourced team to completely manage the soon-to-be-phased-out final assembly line.

After reviewing every job and step in the process, we determined that out of fifteen positions on this assembly line, only three functions were core. Accordingly, MAU assumed responsibility for the remaining twelve.

During the ramp-down, which ultimately lasted nine months, our outsourced team surpassed all of our customer's prior production and quality records. This supports my posi-

Figure 8. Project Design Flowchart

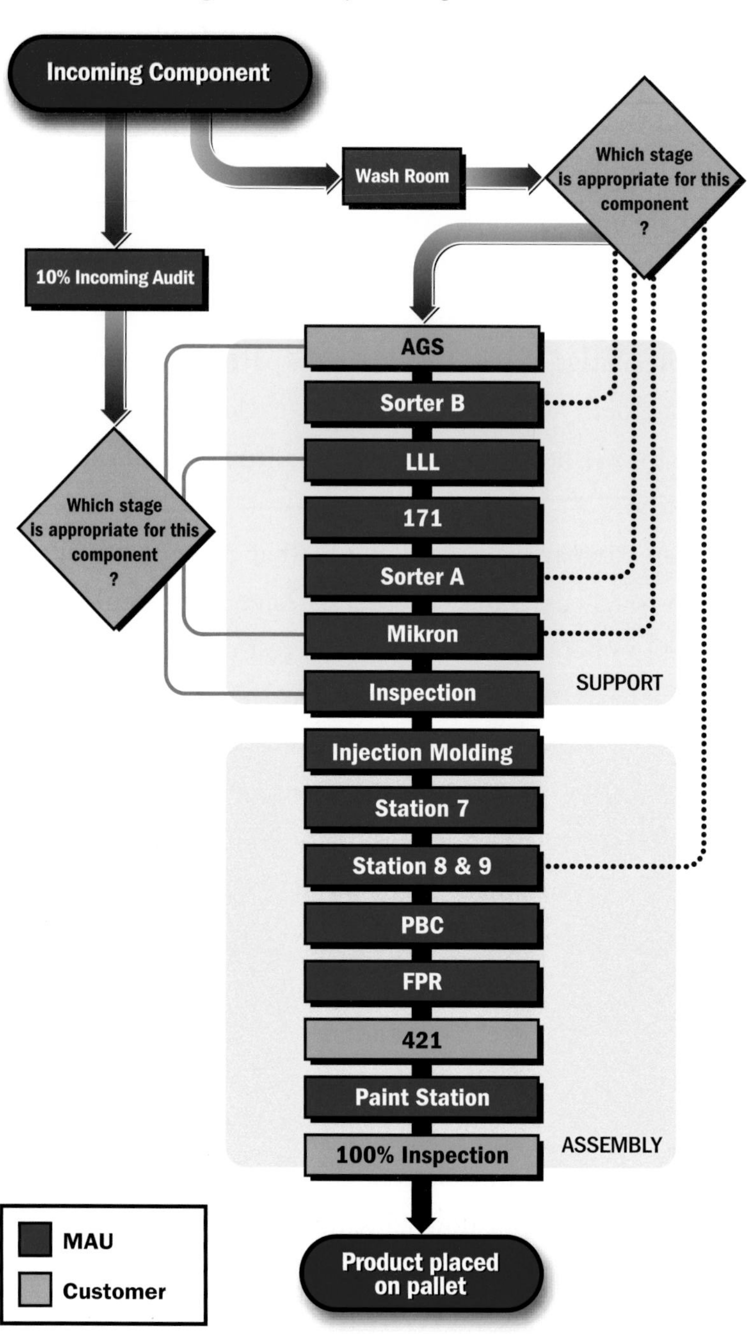

tion that third-party service providers can manage important processes in your company as well as you can. In most cases, they will operate them more efficiently and economically, considering it is not just another department or line to them—their contract is at stake.

Six months after this project was completed, I met with the North American president of this Tier 1 manufacturer and told him we had saved his company approximately $750,000 while beating his historical production and quality standards. He responded to me, "Randy, I realize you did all of that, but the most important thing you did was give us a new tool to put in our toolbox—a new tool for operating our business and making us more competitive."

The Absenteeism-Pool Program

Most companies carry somewhere between 4 and 8 percent in fixed labor costs to cover both planned and unplanned absenteeism, such as vacations, holidays, personal days, and leave programs. As if that percentage weren't high enough already, companies also have to pay overtime to cover absences. When a company accumulates those costs over ten to twenty-five years, think of the legacy debt it must absorb just so employees can take time off. Who can afford that? Once again, business leaders are reading from the old blueprint.

Imagine replacing that fixed headcount with a variable-cost contract group available 24/7 in a just-in-time manner to accommodate planned and unplanned absences as well as rapid changes in production schedules. These cross-trained teams can perform in multiple job competencies across many depart-

Figure 9. Absenteeism Coverage Flowchart

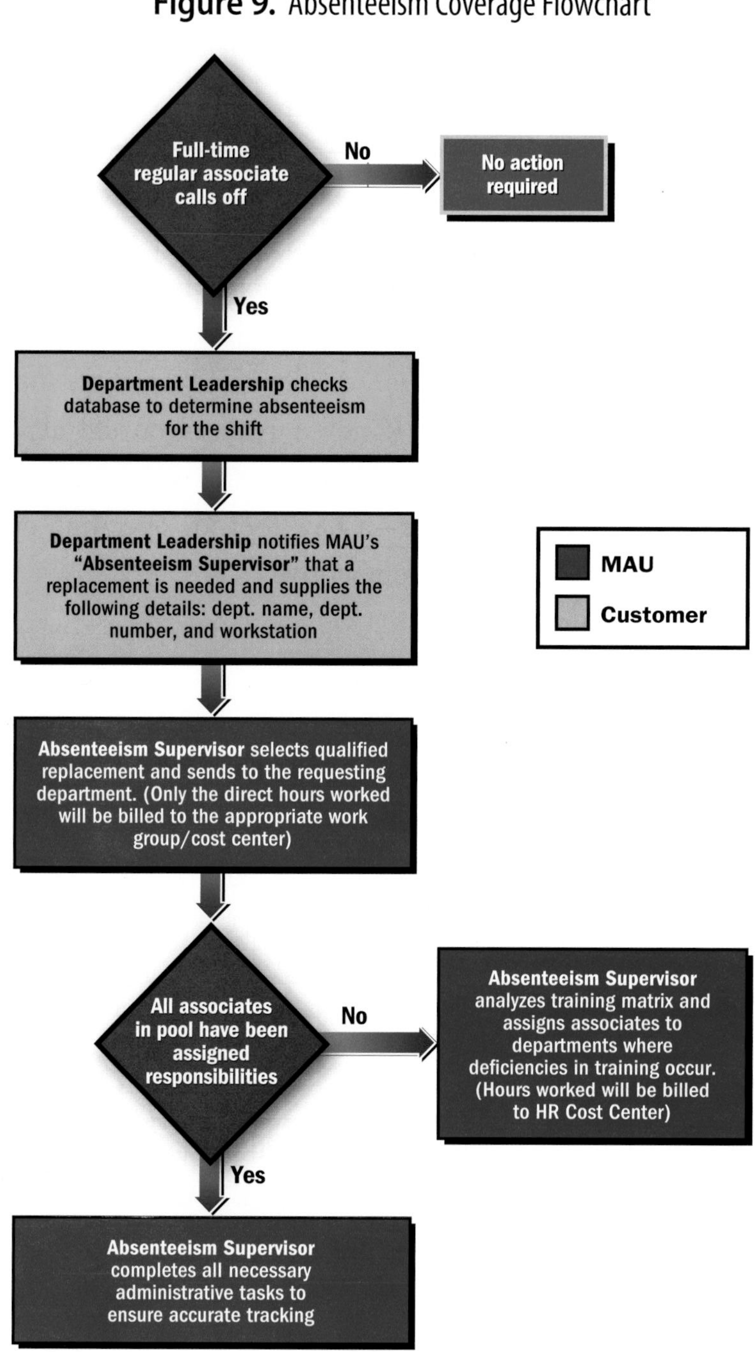

ments, making them highly versatile and effective. Just think of how you could utilize such a skilled, ever-ready SWAT workforce to help you better manage your business.

MAU first developed such a program for a southeastern Tier 1 manufacturer. As our customer struggled to compete with their rivals and their own sister plants, they scrutinized every cost. No one had been willing to reduce full-time headcount, but now everything was on the table. We assembled a team of cross-trained individuals who could handle the tasks within most departments. Our strategy was to give our customer the resources to produce more quality parts at a lower cost. These were our objectives:

- Reduce overtime outlays
- Remove head-count "buffers" and run lean
- Cover absenteeism in real time
- Boost productivity
- Avoid burnout by improving family-work balance for full-time employees

We achieved these goals by designing the process flowchart shown on page 58 (fig. 9).

Our approach yielded staggering results. With only twenty-five MAU associates in this absenteeism pool, we were able to bring the customer an annual savings of $1.1 million. Here's what two department leaders had to say:

> "Since the introduction of this pool, my point leader has been able to react more effectively, backfilling absent

associates at the start of the shift. By using specifically trained contractors, we have achieved even greater production gains."

"Being able to backfill absenteeism with knowledgeable associates has increased output, in addition to reducing potential misbuilds."

Takeaways

- By relying on external providers to manage pilot programs, you can avoid interrupting existing operations and committing your organization to long-term, fixed costs before the new product is proven successful.
- You can better manage ramp-ups and ramp-downs with the tools and resources an outsourcing partner can provide.
- To slash the employee legacy debt associated with absenteeism and improve responsiveness to organizational leaders, companies can turn to ever-ready, cross-trained contract teams.

THIRTEEN

Make Your Equipment Hum

As one way to optimize manufacturing assets, business leaders are seriously looking at transferring maintenance responsibilities to external service providers. AMR Research, a well-known manufacturing research company, recently reported, "As companies look to reduce total maintenance costs, improve overall equipment effectiveness (OEE), and proactively manage the issue of the graying workforce, outsourcing maintenance must be an option explored." According to Jeff Owens, President of Advanced Technology Services (ATS), a leading third-party supplier of production maintenance, "Outsourcing maintenance can increase asset productivity by as much as 30 percent in factories where maintenance is not considered a core competency." Owens adds, "But the decision to outsource must be strategic for it to succeed."

Indeed, maintenance is gaining attention because unlike in the past, companies are now viewing it as strategic. Maintenance workers are called many names around a plant—fix-it guys, firefighters, technical wizards (to name a few flattering ones)—but they're seldom considered strategic partners. This is changing as more and more top executives insist on a workable maintenance plan that aligns with the overall corporate vision. Vague objectives, such as "we will increase effectiveness of the maintenance department," are inadequate; organizations must pair accurate, realistic measures with achievable improvement goals.

Be honest—do you view maintenance as a necessary evil? Do you believe it's an uncontrollable cost? If so, you could be missing an important productivity opportunity. In his book *Computerized Maintenance Management Services* (2nd ed., Industrial Press, 1994), Terry Wireman states that most internal maintenance groups are only 33 percent productive.

Inefficiency, though, should not be the driving factor behind shopping for third-party suppliers. You must first determine if your in-house maintenance adds any value to your product or service. Remember, identifying your core functions doesn't mean assessing what you do well and what you do poorly. Rather, you need to pinpoint the activities you must do yourself if you're going to gain a competitive edge in your market—and outsource the rest.

If you decide that maintenance is a noncore-critical function for your business, you can actually gain greater overall control when you transfer it to an experienced service provider. But it's important to define the word "control" here. Does it mean dictating what tasks maintenance workers perform every day and how they must do them? Or does it mean making sure your key machines have top priority? Ultimately, we need to define "control" in terms of activities and results. If you aren't achieving maintenance objectives, how much control do you really have? When outsourcing maintenance, you will definitely lose some direct control of the tasks involved, but you will gain much more control of maintenance outcomes.

Without data, you can't proactively drive results. Third parties must present performance metrics to justify their contract and demonstrate continuous improvement. This information allows senior executives to make fact-based decisions about widespread problems, machines requiring excessive maintenance dollars, and asset upgrades or replacements.

I'm sure many of you are wondering why you'd even consider outsourcing maintenance since it's so critical. Yes, effective maintenance is key to the success of any lean manufacturer, but executives must also utilize predictive and preventive approaches to address sophisticated delivery requirements. For many plants, though, internal factors prevent them from making critical improvements to their maintenance programs. An external provider can sidestep these barriers to ensure that the right equipment is working at the right time to produce the right results.

Outsourcing the maintenance on your production equipment offers the following benefits:

- Immediate access to the most advanced maintenance technologies available in the world
- The ability to learn from people who eat, drink, and sleep maintenance

- Exposure to maintenance professionals who possess significant experience in transforming weak maintenance groups into high-performance ones
- Enhanced opportunities for personal and career growth as the outsourcing company assimilates your maintenance team into their organization

Now you can understand why this outsourcing application is receiving so much attention. As you embrace such a progressive, much-needed business concept, you will gain the immediate support of senior management, and your existing maintenance employees will eventually learn that you have created new avenues for them to progress professionally.

Takeaways

- As executives change the way they manage all their business functions, they have begun viewing maintenance workers as strategic partners.
- To benefit fully from outsourcing their in-house maintenance, leaders must determine that this function is not linked to their core business.
- By contracting a facility-maintenance service provider, companies can gain access to continuous data, make more-informed decisions about equipment, and increase productivity by almost a third.

FOURTEEN

The Future Is Here

Consolidating all the concepts we have discussed, MAU's **Innovative Workforce Model** offers a twenty-first-century method for conducting business. Companies can now enjoy the stability of full-time employees and the fluidity and affordability of a flexible workforce, combined with the additional stability and fluidity of qualified outsourcing resources.

The evolution of the workforce can be best understood in the following manner. The Staffing Workforce Model (fig.2) included a flexible workforce that grouped together temporary staffers, contract workers, co-ops, and interns. In the Innovative Workforce Model (fig. 10), just the temporary workers remain in this category, and the others are now managed by outsourced partners.

Today, temporary workers are largely responsible for responding to business fluctuations and specialty projects in both core and noncore areas. The outsourced workers are more

Figure 10. Innovative Workforce Model

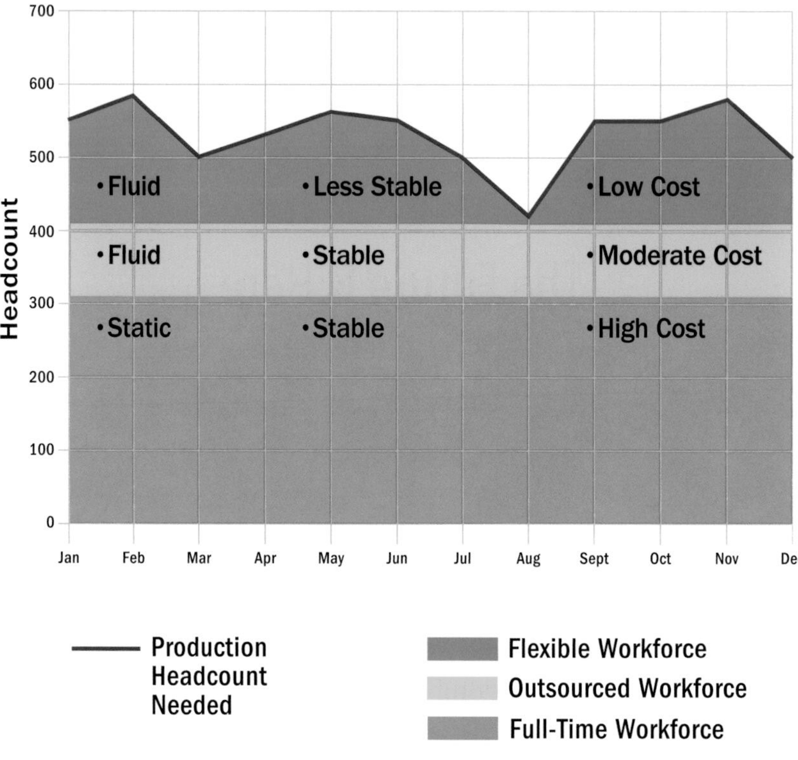

Workforce	Headcount											
	Jan	Feb	Mar	Apr	May	June	July	Aug	Sept	Oct	Nov	Dec
Flexible*	140	170	90	120	150	140	90	15	140	140	170	90
Outsourced†	100	100	100	100	100	100	100	100	100	100	100	100
Full-Time	310	310	310	310	310	310	310	310	310	310	310	310
Total	550	580	500	530	560	550	500	425	550	550	580	500
Production	**550**	**580**	**500**	**530**	**560**	**550**	**500**	**425**	**550**	**550**	**580**	**500**

*Temporary workers only, hired to accommodate business fluctuations in both core and noncore areas.

†Includes co-ops, interns, and contract workers managed by outsourced partners. Responsible for noncore activities.

stable because they oversee noncore activities that were historically a full-time regular function or process.

The transformative, strategic approach of the Innovative Workforce Model requires a moderate cost increase from the Staffing Workforce Model because you can now access new management services, technology, and expertise. In most cases, though, your operating costs will decrease and your company will become more focused and efficient.

What is your optimal number of full-time, flexible, and outsourced employees? Some companies have traditionally chosen arbitrary numbers—for example, a temporary workforce of no more than 15 percent of the total. Those figures will likely change because the company and its outsourced partners will decide themselves on the amount of temporary help each will use. Also, it is possible that some of the historically more critical temporary jobs will be converted to full-time jobs in outsourced functions. Whether you follow some mathematical formula—such as balancing the number of full-time versus temporary and outsourced employees—or simply make a plan based on your best-guess economic and market forecasts, it will be your willingness and need to change that will most influence your final decisions on how to move forward.

Innovative Workforce Model:

Full-time employees, a flexible workforce consisting of temp workers only, and outsourced partners

An example I'd like to share involves a customer of ours, a southeastern manufacturer that had essentially been using the Staffing Workforce Model for many years. We proposed to

Figure 11. Innovative Workforce Savings
Southeast Manufacturer

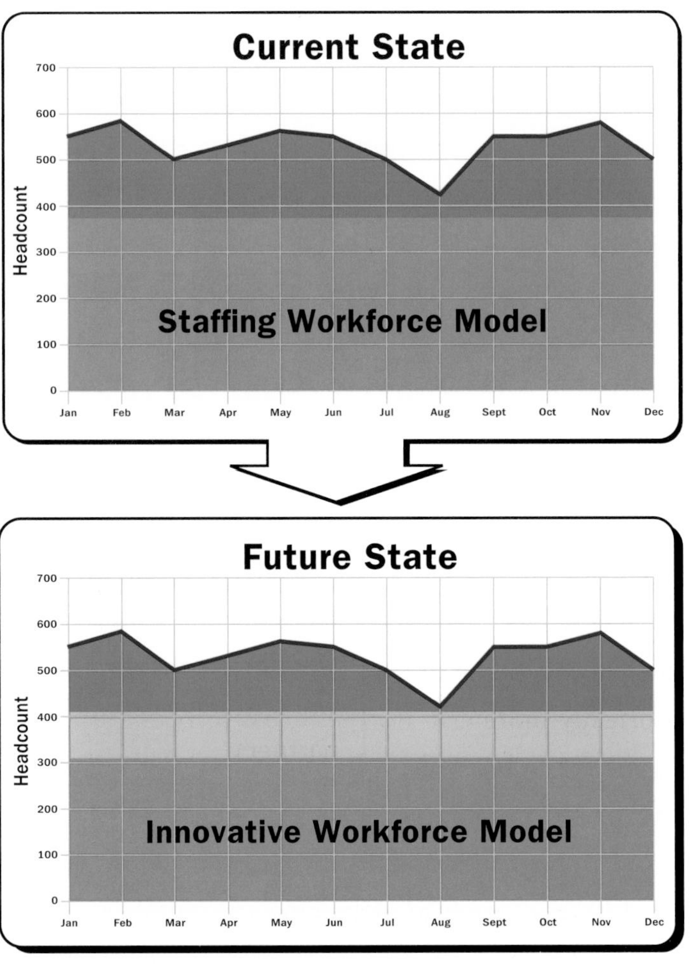

	Current State Investment	Future State Investment	Savings
Year 1	$20,638,559	$18,069,272	$2,569,287
Year 5	$103,192,796	$90,346,360	$12,846,436
Year 10	**$206,385,592**	**$180,692,719**	**$25,692,873**

them the concept of transferring a number of their functions to external service providers. To illustrate the benefits of such a move, we compared their current model with an outsourced one and estimated the ROI they would realize over the next ten years (fig. 11). By year 10 of implementing these changes, our customer was projected to save over $25 million while sharpening their focus on core functions.

In 1990, Charles Handy predicted in *The Age of Unreason* (Harvard Business School Press) that our workforces would morph into a two-group system: (1) full-time employees managing 50 percent of the company resources, services, and talents (core), and (2) third-party suppliers managing the remaining 50 percent (noncore). Handy explained that this progression had already occurred in Europe. So it made sense that the rest of the world would evolve in the same way.

Four years later in 1994, Handy admitted in *The Age of Paradox* (Harvard Business School Press) that some of what he had written in his previous book had been fairly optimistic. He went on to say that the world of business had changed much more than he'd ever expected.

What would he say today about the changes since then? Consider the macro effects of globalism: tariffs, cheap labor, government influence, technology, currency exchange rates, and so on. Business has become much more complex and competitive. According to a recent IBM study of more than 1,500 CEOs worldwide, "private and public sector leaders believe that a rapid escalation of 'complexity' is the biggest challenge confronting them. . . . [and] that their enterprises today are not equipped to cope effectively."

Yet in their eagerness—or desperation—to find solutions, companies must not underestimate the value of human relationships. For example, if efficiency in a corporation became in and of itself the goal, rather than a means to an end, the people side of the equation would be lost.

I've noticed that as they embark on outsourcing relationships, many international companies have suffered from choosing poorly in this area. In good faith, executives embrace an outsourcing solution that in some instances involves a global process or platform. Not surprisingly, they struggle with fully understanding these complex projects, making them vulnerable to providers that overpromise their capabilities.

Corporate sales teams with ghost souls gain access to the CEO's staff members and tell them they can drive more money and efficiency to their bottom line. In short order, these so-called partners have ravaged company systems and processes, frequently damaging the internal culture and reputation and adversely affecting the quality and delivery of the product or service offered.

So take the time to find a partner you can trust. An often-overused word, trust forms the basis of any outsourced relationship. You must have confidence in the company and the people you are discussing a partnership with—your company's future success lies in the balance. Equally important is ensuring they have expertly performed the entire scope of services they are promising to deliver.

Trusted partners don't always have to be the final solution. I learned about many of the concepts described in this book from companies that are now our partners. We help one another by introducing our respective customers to the best resources in the world. Find partners willing to not only provide their services but also expose you to firms with services they don't provide. Although no one outsource-solutions company does it all, some—like MAU—are strategically positioned with other outsourcers to bring you a greater return on your investment.

I recommend working with partners amenable to designing and implementing their solutions at a measured pace that will protect your culture and provide for thoughtful, ongoing evaluation of the management and control of your business functions. Commit to choosing third parties that will have a positive effect on your product or service, employees, and customers.

Though I am still urging caution, now is the time to make your move. Your competitors are already moving in this direction or soon will be. I implore you not to wait for the future—because I believe the *future is already here.*

Takeaways

- Combining all the workforce concepts, MAU's Innovative Workforce Model provides the fluidity, stability, affordability, and—most importantly—the focus that organizations need to succeed in the twenty-first century.
- As they pursue greater efficiencies and profits, executives must not lose sight of the value of trusted relationships.
- Choose external providers with care and outsource in a systematic way that preserves your company's culture while achieving the needed change.

FIFTEEN

A 10,000-Hour Focus

In his best-selling book *The Outliers* (Little, Brown and Company, 2008), Malcolm Gladwell talks about what he calls the "10,000-Hour Rule." According to the author, in order for many high achievers to get their first big break, they must invest at least 10,000 hours in what I call their core competency. Here are three examples:

- Bill Joy: He rewrote both Java and the UNIX Operating System, and cofounded Sun Microsystems. Before achieving success, he programmed—his core competency—for 10,000 hours.

- The Beatles: Can you imagine how many different instruments you would have to play and different song sets you would have to know to play on stage five to six hours every night for almost five years? You would need incredible range and depth in instruments, vocals, and lyrics because

Figure 12. The Goal: 10,000-Hour Focus

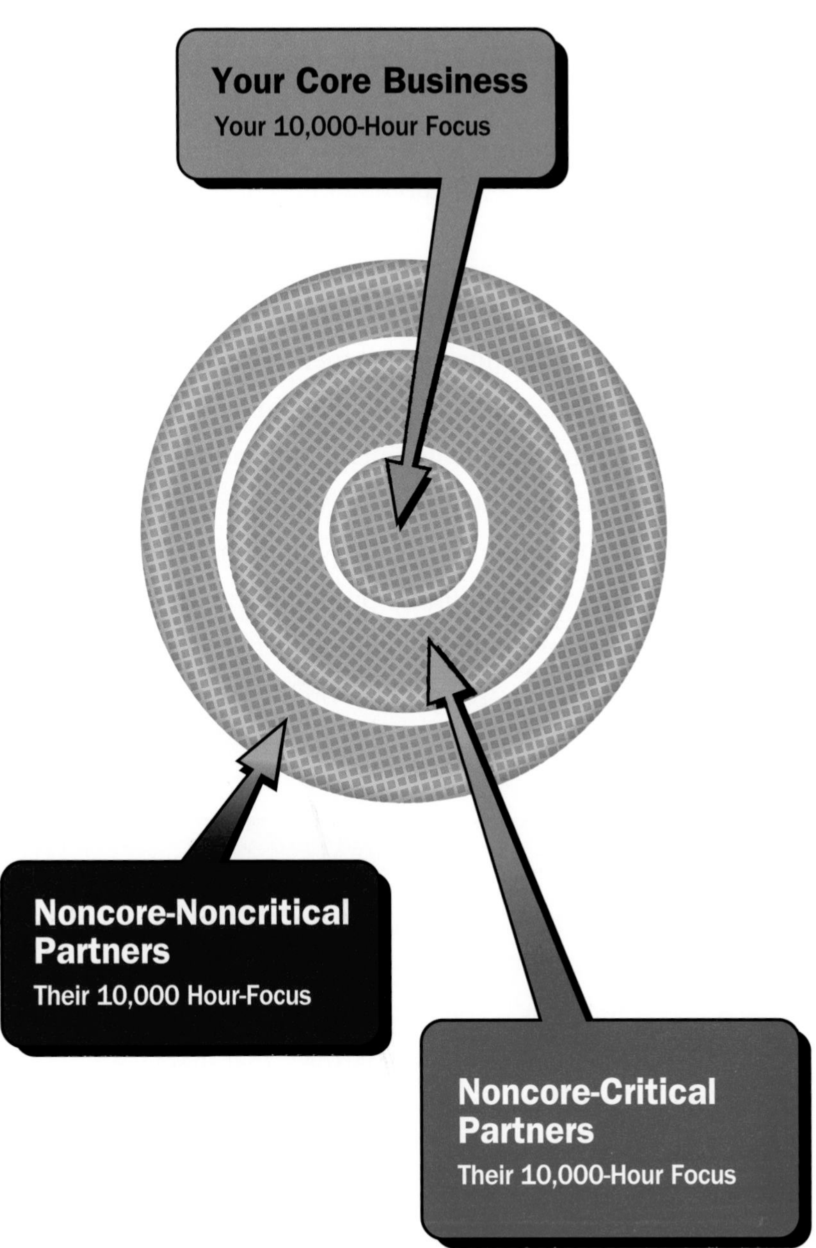

you couldn't repeat the same songs and sound all the time. Before coming to the United States in 1964, the Beatles had accumulated well over 10,000 hours in their core competency: live musical performance.

- Bill Gates: Programming since the seventh grade, Gates had clocked over 10,000 hours in his core competency before he dropped out of Harvard and started Microsoft.

Visualize your whole company humming with this 10,000-hour focus (fig. 12). Your noncore partners, with their 10,000-hour focus, are shining the toilets, hiring new employees, manicuring the grounds, optimizing equipment utilization, streamlining product movement, and integrating error-free financial services.

In the meantime, your managers, with their 10,000-hour core focus, are creating and designing products and services, driving higher-efficiency improvements, closing a merger, and meeting face-to-face with a new customer to promote your latest offering.

A winning strategy!

Takeaways

- Commit to making your entire organization operate with a 10,000-hour core focus.
- Drive growth and profitability by outsourcing your noncore functions to trusted partners that share your highly targeted focus.
- When companies strategically transform their labor blueprint, they can move closer to performing at 100 percent core competency.

Utopia

Ray Meads smiled as he looked over his year-end board of directors' book that included his consolidated financial statements for the 200 plants he now operated worldwide. The profit numbers were staggering, but more amazing to him was the journey that had brought him to this point. Ray was truly an executive who had reinvented himself. He had relentlessly searched the world for best-of-class practices and concepts that challenged all the sacred cows of his company, subjecting him to much criticism and conjecture, not to mention the possibility of failure.

Now his critics were silent, and quite frankly most of them were no longer with the company. That's because there wasn't a lot of room in Ray's company anymore for layers of management and infrastructure. A mere eight people made up corporate: Ray the president, his VPs of finance, human resources, engineering, sales, quality, manufacturing, and R&D. There were no staff functions below them and no organizational dynasty charts. After all, why would you need a lot of corporate structure for an executive leadership team whose sole responsibility was managing strategic partnerships?

Ray's plants were now being operated by partners that in turn had strategic partners handling all their noncore processes. At both the corporate and the plant level, his finance and accounting functions were managed through a global outsourced platform that accommodated the twenty-two countries in which he operated 24/7. The members of his executive team were free to work together on a day-to-day basis focusing on new products and offerings, and implementing sales strategies to ensure they outpaced any competitive threats. The only corporate employees existing beyond this level were those in the sales function who jumped on planes and maintained face-to-face relationships with current and prospective clientele.

As Ray flipped through the rest of the tabs in the board book he'd be presenting to the directors in two weeks, he could hardly contain himself:

- **Quality**. They virtually had no competition—no other company in the world was exceeding his quality ratings.
- **Efficiency**. He was constantly producing more product faster and utilizing less and less of the company's capital to do so.
- **Human Resources**. It had been three years since any lawsuits, and there was no need for a report about escalating compensation and benefit costs since just the executive team and the sales force remained.

- **Public Relations**. The last tab was the best. Ray reread with pride the stories from the *Wall Street Journal*, *Business Week*, *Fortune*, and others—the list was five pages long. It contained all the television, podcast, blog, and radio appearances he had made over the last year as the corporate world tried to understand how he had accomplished such a business phenomenon so quickly.

Ray was startled by the ringing telephone, and as he reached to answer it, he saw the name of the caller displayed: his CEO. They had to schedule a time to review the materials for the board meeting. Ray wouldn't share everything with his boss, however. No, he wouldn't reveal his most controversial agenda item until the last session of the board meeting.

At that point, they would begin discussing Ray's recommendation that the CEO's position be eliminated—because it was no longer needed.

Dream on. Dream big. Most of all, *never waste a crisis.*

Takeaways at a Glance

One How Good is Great

- Past greatness does not guarantee a company's future.
- In the years to come, thriving businesses will know how to manage every part of their organization with excellence.
- The most successful executives will concentrate a majority of their time and resources on what will keep their companies growing and prospering in the decades ahead.

Two It Could Happen to You

- Have you made many business changes over the years but found your market share still slipping?
- Are you constantly making excuses to avoid addressing the high price tag and inefficiencies of your full-time regular workforce?
- Are you afraid to eliminate any of your sacred cows?

Three The Corporate Family

- According to the first labor blueprint, the Patriarchal Workforce Model, people assumed that they'd be working for one company their entire lives.
- Huge corporate profits masked the escalating compensation and benefit costs that were generating a long-term employee legacy debt.
- Having only a static labor force at their disposal, employers had no effective staffing solutions for marketplace expansions and contractions.

Four The 1970s Bring Flexibility

- The seeds of the temporary workforce were planted during WWII.
- Maturing in the 1970s, the Staffing Workforce Model combined full-time employees with a flexible workforce consisting of temporary and contract workers, co-ops, and interns.
- Companies could now balance labor and production levels while converting some of the fixed labor costs to variable ones and mitigating employee liabilities.

Five Hidden Costs of Temp Workers

- While companies have realized tremendous cost savings by utilizing a temporary workforce, they have unknowingly forfeited many of those savings in wasteful, unmeasured ways.
- Over time, the compensation and benefit gap between temporary and full-time workers has widened.
- You must determine a current market valuation of wages and benefit scales for both temporary and full-time workers, especially if you hire from the temporary group.

Six Paying the Piper

- Employee legacy costs, once a speck on the distant horizon, have grown proportionally too large for today's businesses to ignore.
- By failing to look at their workforces strategically, companies have become less competitive in the global marketplace.
- Although the Patriarchal and Staffing models were once effective, their incomplete designs, combined with the economic crisis, are insufficient alone to address the complex needs of twenty-first-century businesses.

Seven A New Business Blueprint

- It sometimes takes an outside perspective to jolt executives into shifting away from a dated, inefficient model and toward a lean one centered on value-added core activities.
- For a number of companies, doing the same thing year after year—despite a steady decline in the marketplace—is better than risking the unknown.
- Many leaders continue to follow their old business blueprint because their packed schedules don't afford them the time to design a new one.

Eight Start Your Journey

- Take a hands-on approach to determining your core and noncore business by walking the floors of your plant and reviewing each function, process, and activity yourself.
- As few as 50 percent of your current jobs, processes, and functions could be classified as core.
- Many noncore activities are candidates for outsourcing to third-party providers, even though they are currently staffed by full-time employees.

Nine If Time Is Money

- What you think about and act on every day affects the short- and long-term outcomes of your business and career.
- Those companies that clearly differentiate between their core functions and those they can turn over to third parties will realize a competitive advantage.
- Business leaders must be willing to make difficult decisions, which can include terminating full-time employees—even those at the top.

Ten HR's New Best Friend

- Growing in popularity, Recruitment Process Outsourcing (RPO) can help HR departments reduce hiring costs while improving efficiency.
- To obtain the most value from RPO, companies need to consider using it for both internal and external workforce movement.
- Co-op and internship initiatives can be significantly enhanced through programs managed by third parties.

Eleven The Company Rudder

- Because CFO responsibilities are expanding in complexity and scope, business leaders must be prudent in managing all resources and expenses.
- By partnering with a Finance and Accounting Outsourcing (FAO) service provider, companies can augment their finance team with global employees trained in customized processes and contractually dedicated to delivering quality services.

- Companies can now transfer day-to-day tasks to a third party at a fraction of the historical cost, giving CFOs the freedom to focus on strategic activities that support the growing business.

Twelve Another Tool for Your Toolbox

- By relying on external providers to manage pilot programs, you can avoid interrupting existing operations and committing your organization to long-term, fixed costs before the new product is proven successful.
- You can better manage ramp-ups and ramp-downs with the tools and resources an outsourcing partner can provide.
- To slash the employee legacy debt associated with absenteeism and improve responsiveness to organizational leaders, companies can turn to ever-ready, cross-trained contract teams.

Thirteen Make Your Equipment Hum

- As executives change the way they manage all their business functions, they have begun viewing maintenance workers as strategic partners.
- To benefit fully from outsourcing their in-house maintenance, leaders must determine that this function is not linked to their core business.
- By contracting a facility-maintenance service provider, companies can gain access to continuous data, make more-informed decisions about equipment, and increase productivity by almost a third.

Fourteen The Future Is Here

- Combining all the workforce concepts, MAU's Innovative Workforce Model provides the fluidity, stability, affordability, and—most importantly—the focus that organizations need to succeed in the twenty-first century.
- As they pursue greater efficiencies and profits, executives must not lose sight of the value of trusted relationships.
- Choose external providers with care and outsource in a systematic way that preserves your company's culture while achieving the needed change.

Fifteen A 10,000-Hour Focus

- Commit to making your entire organization operate with a 10,000-hour core focus.
- Drive growth and profitability by outsourcing your noncore functions to trusted partners that share your highly targeted focus.
- When companies strategically transform their labor blueprint, they can move closer to performing at 100 percent core competency.

Workforce Toolkit

Figure 1. Patriarchal Workforce Model

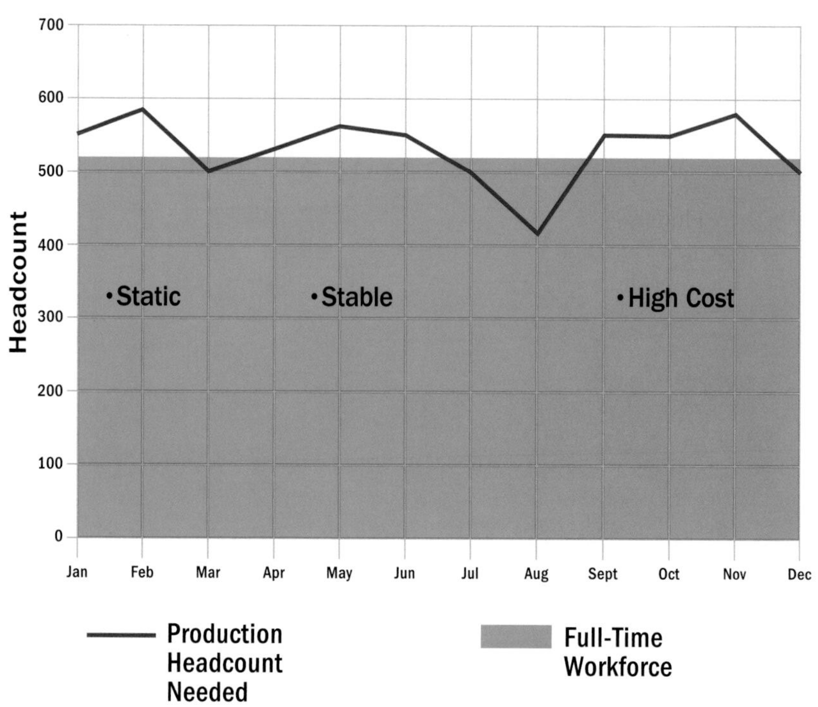

Workforce	Headcount											
	Jan	Feb	Mar	Apr	May	June	July	Aug	Sept	Oct	Nov	Dec
Full-Time	520	520	520	520	520	520	520	520	520	520	520	520
Production	**550**	**580**	**500**	**530**	**560**	**550**	**500**	**425**	**550**	**550**	**580**	**500**
Δ	-30	-60	+20	-10	-40	-30	+20	+95	-30	-30	-60	+20

Figure 2. Staffing Workforce Model

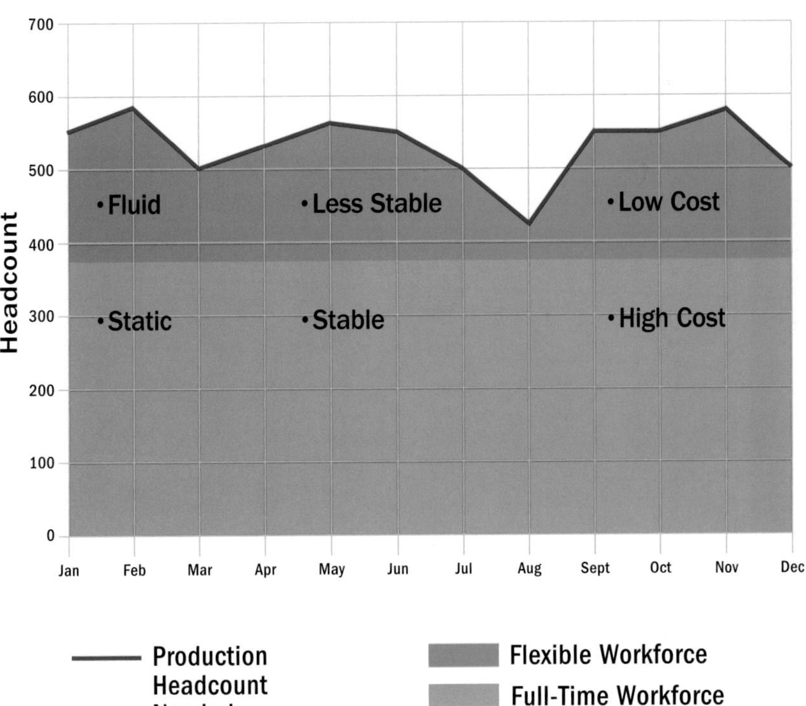

Workforce	Headcount											
	Jan	Feb	Mar	Apr	May	June	July	Aug	Sept	Oct	Nov	Dec
Flexible*	175	205	125	155	185	175	125	50	175	175	205	125
Full-Time	375	375	375	375	375	375	375	375	375	375	375	375
Total	550	580	500	530	560	550	500	425	550	550	580	500
Production	**550**	**580**	**500**	**530**	**560**	**550**	**500**	**425**	**550**	**550**	**580**	**500**

*Temporary and contract workers, co-ops, and interns.

Figure 10. Innovative Workforce Model

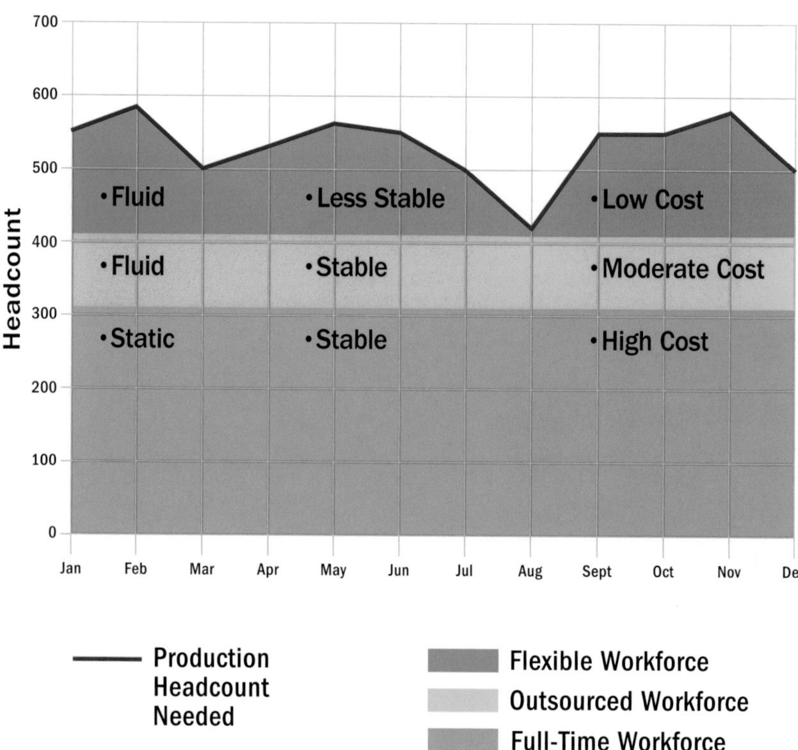

Production Headcount Needed

Flexible Workforce

Outsourced Workforce

Full-Time Workforce

Workforce	Headcount											
	Jan	Feb	Mar	Apr	May	June	July	Aug	Sept	Oct	Nov	Dec
Flexible*	140	170	90	120	150	140	90	15	140	140	170	90
Outsourced †	100	100	100	100	100	100	100	100	100	100	100	100
Full-Time	310	310	310	310	310	310	310	310	310	310	310	310
Total	550	580	500	530	560	550	500	425	550	550	580	500
Production	**550**	**580**	**500**	**530**	**560**	**550**	**500**	**425**	**550**	**550**	**580**	**500**

*Temporary workers only, hired to accommodate business fluctuations in both core and noncore areas.

†Includes co-ops, interns, and contract workers managed by outsourced partners. Responsible for noncore activities.

Figure 11. Innovative Workforce Savings
Southeast Manufacturer

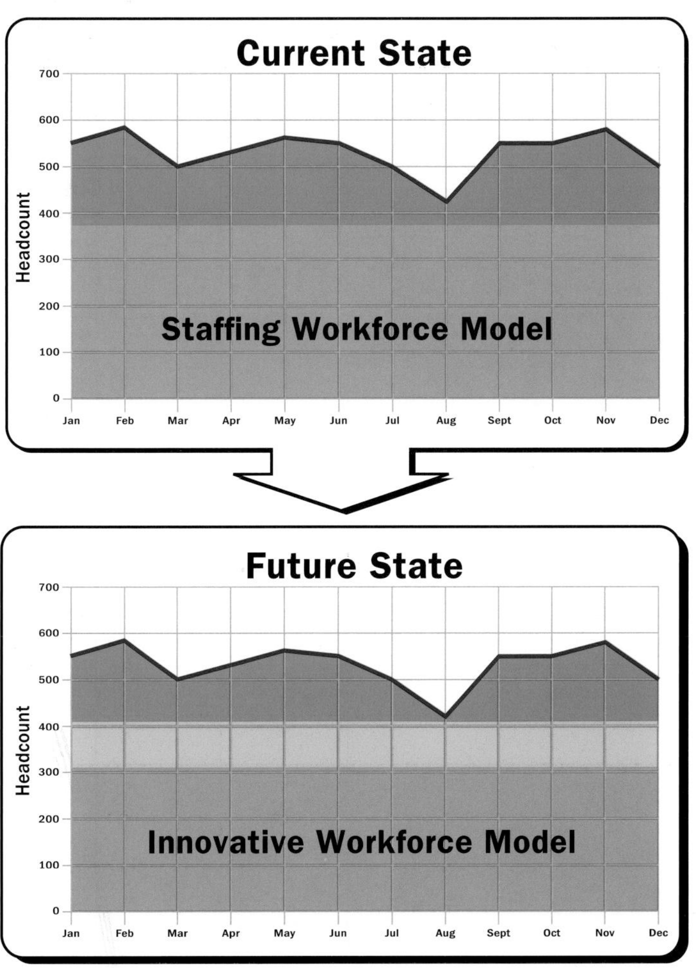

	Current State Investment	Future State Investment	Savings
Year 1	$20,638,559	$18,069,272	$2,569,287
Year 5	$103,192,796	$90,346,360	$12,846,436
Year 10	**$206,385,592**	**$180,692,719**	**$25,692,873**

Figure 3. Core/Noncore Walk-Through

Job Title/Function	Core	Noncore	
		Critical	Noncritical

Visit http://www.mau.com/resources for a downloadable, interactive form you can use.

Figure 4. Core/Noncore Analysis

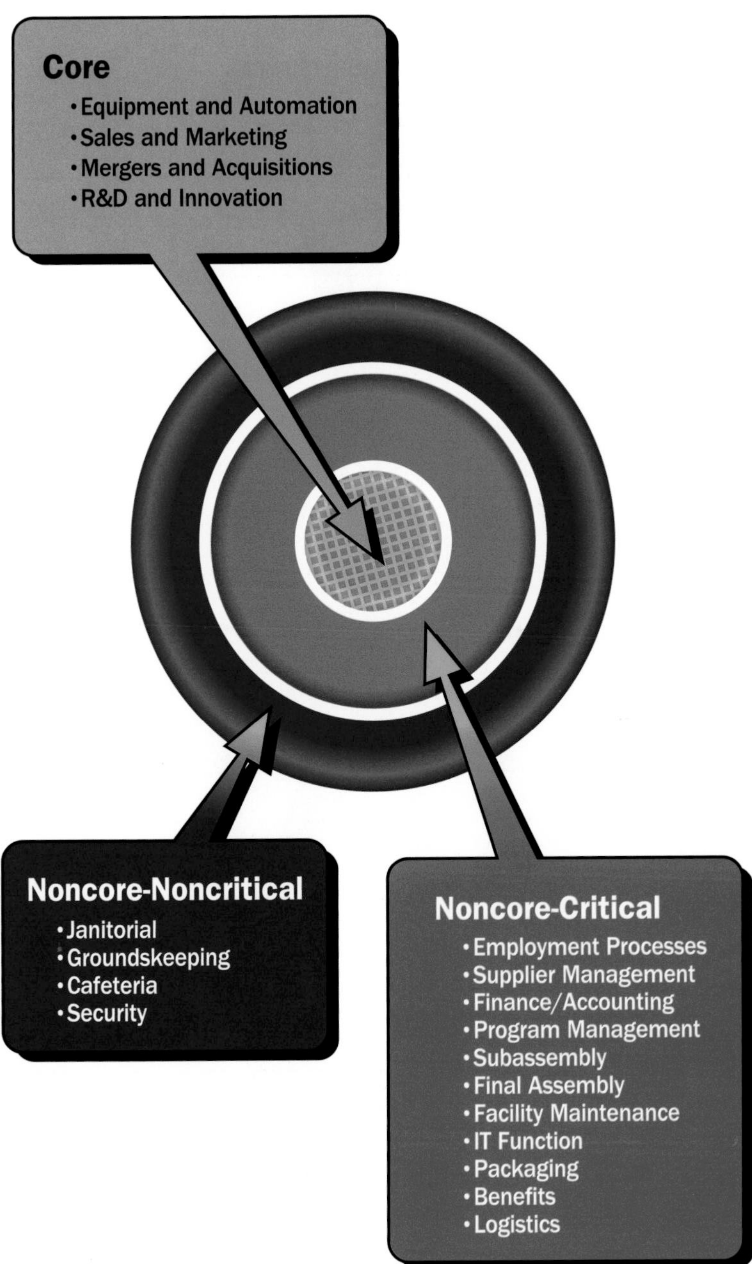

Figure 12. The Goal: 10,000-Hour Focus

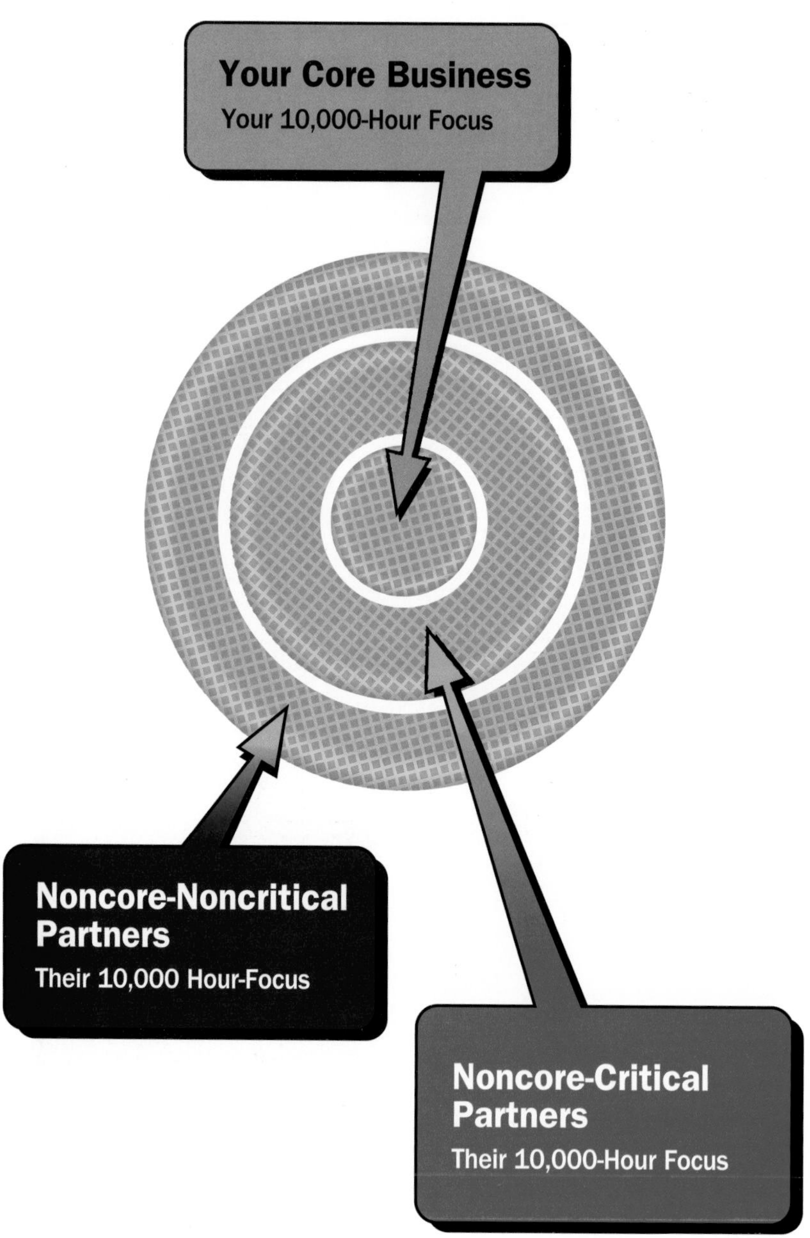

Figure 5. External Recruiting Process Outsourcing
Sales & Marketing

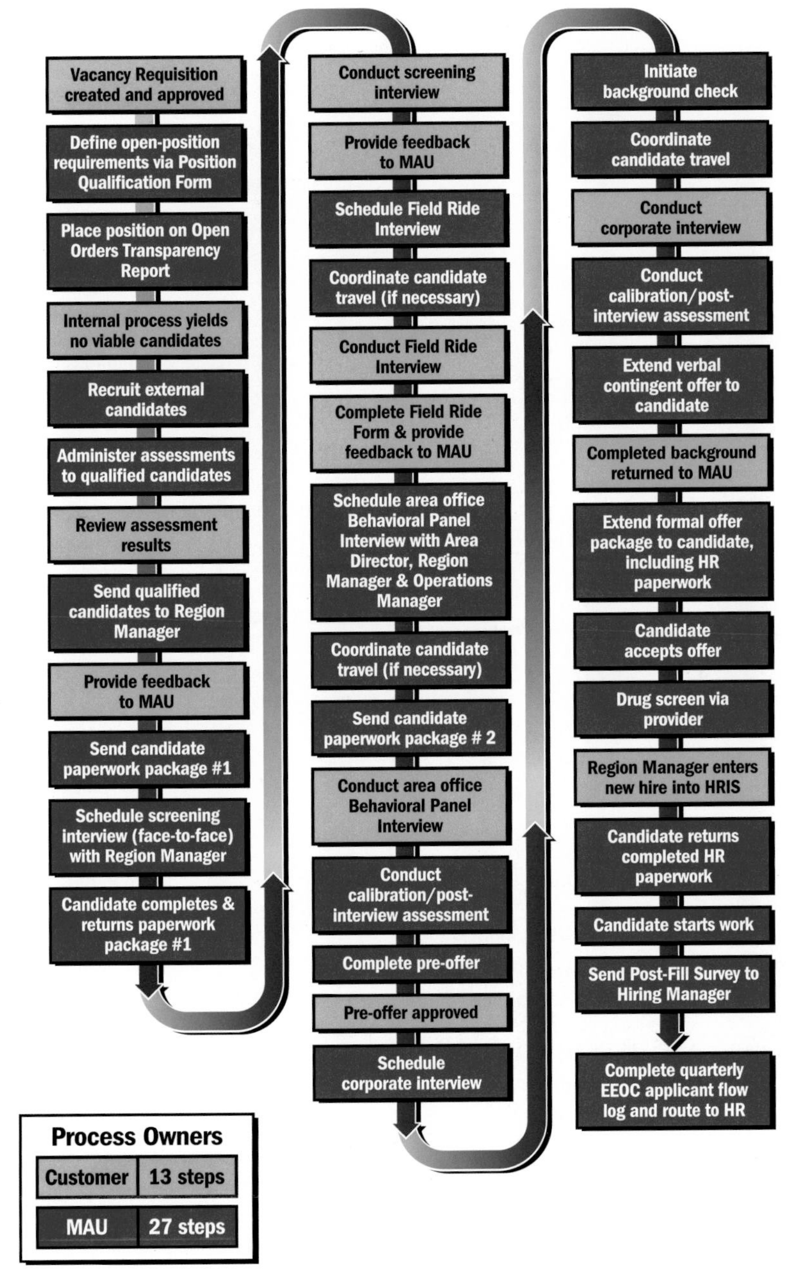

Process Owners

Customer	13 steps
MAU	27 steps

Figure 6. Finance & Accounting Outsourcing

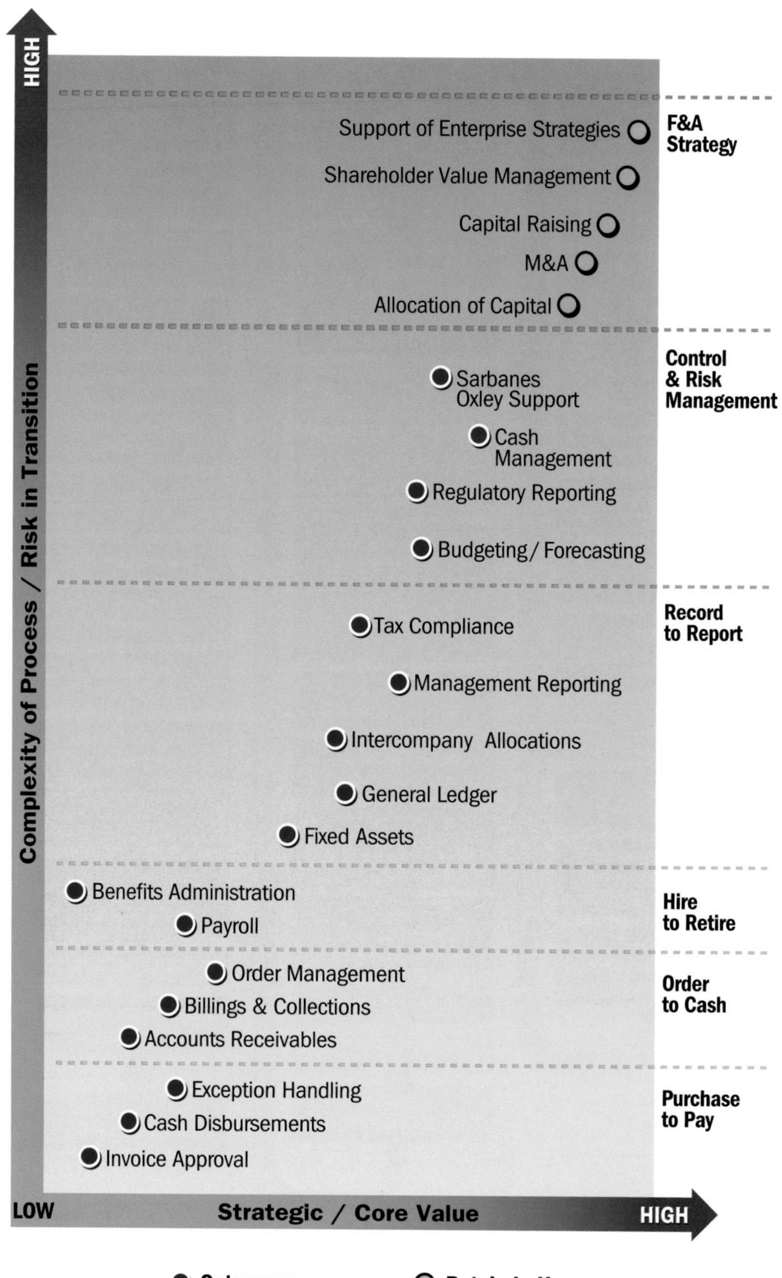

Figure 7. Kit Assembly Process

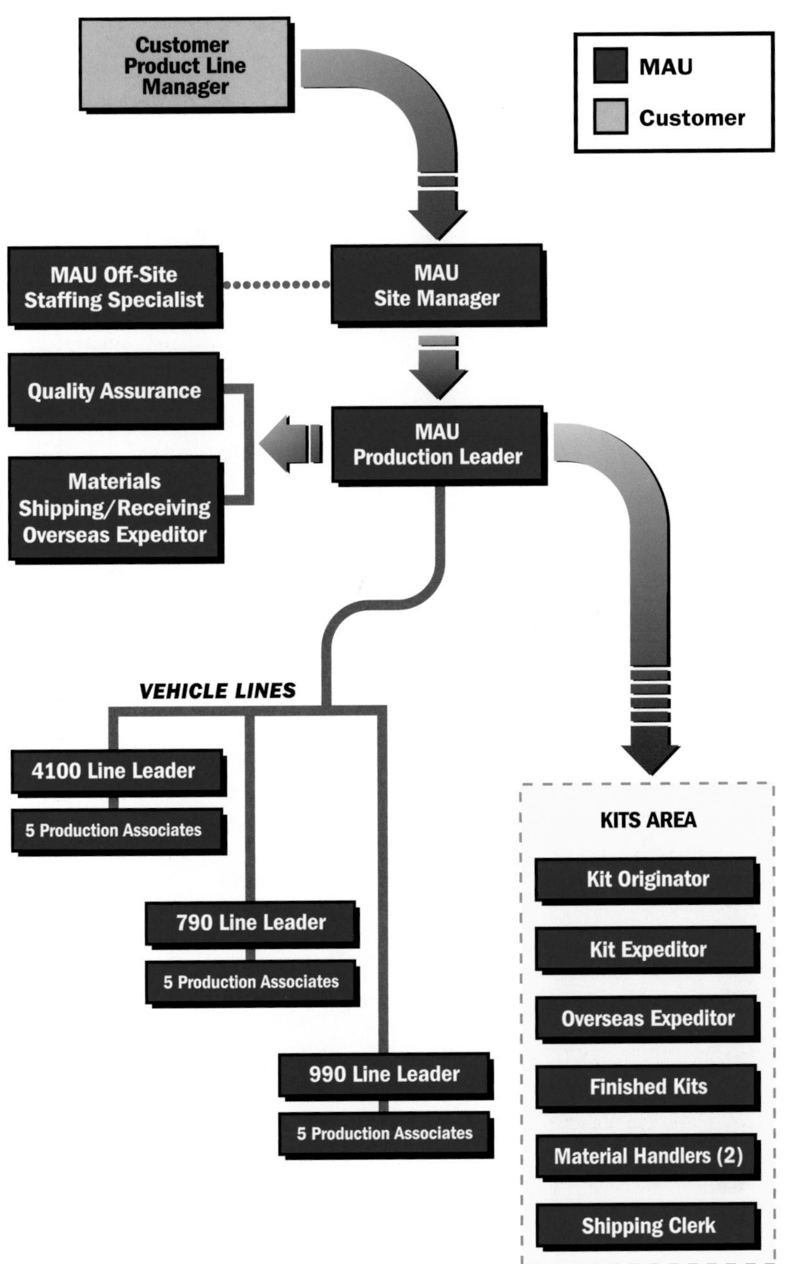

Figure 8. Project Design Flowchart

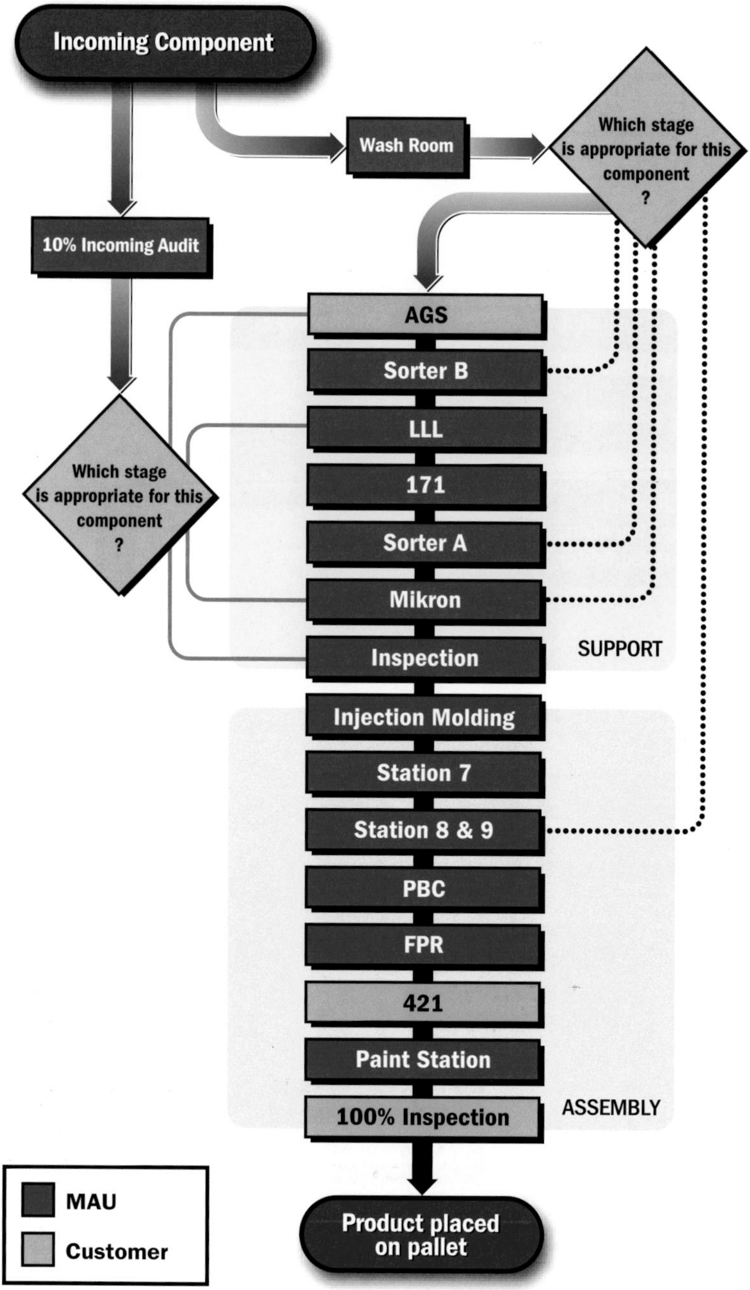

Incoming Component

Wash Room

Which stage is appropriate for this component ?

10% Incoming Audit

Which stage is appropriate for this component ?

AGS

Sorter B

LLL

171

Sorter A

Mikron

Inspection

SUPPORT

Injection Molding

Station 7

Station 8 & 9

PBC

FPR

421

Paint Station

100% Inspection

ASSEMBLY

Product placed on pallet

MAU

Customer

Figure 9. Absenteeism Coverage Flowchart

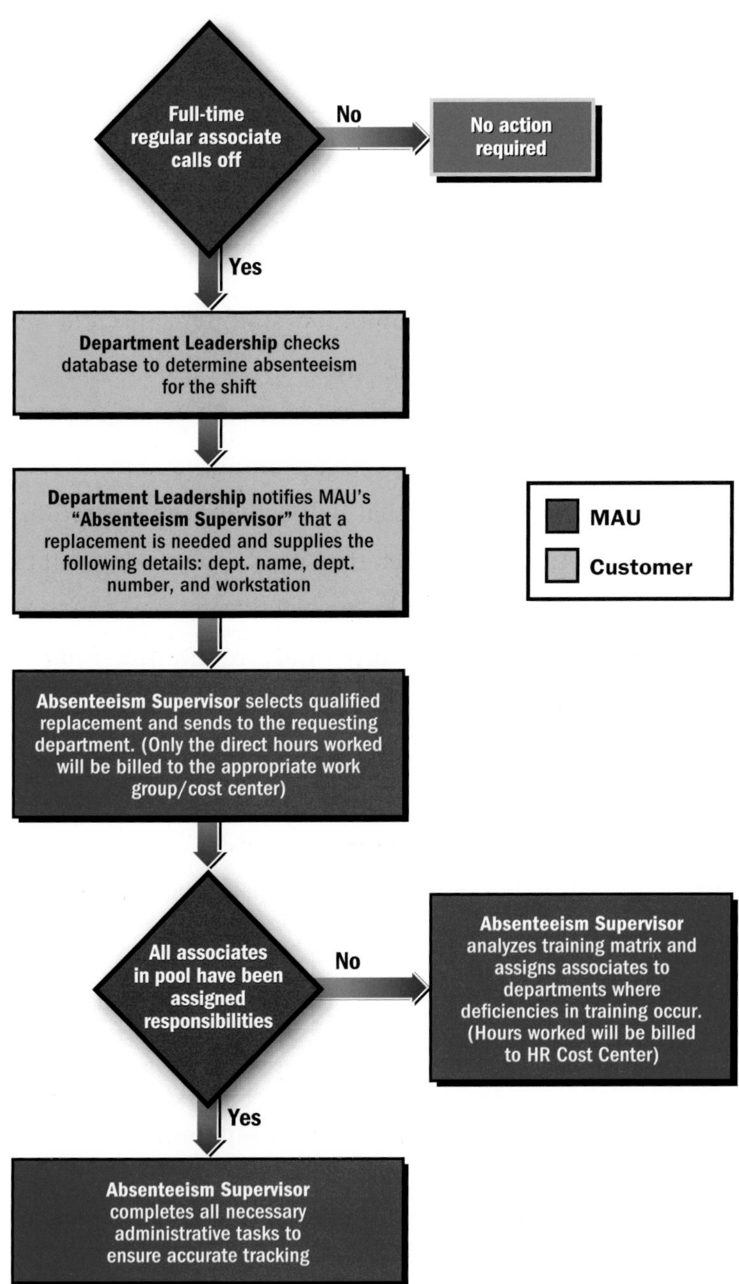

Many Factors to Consider

Managers with service-level responsibility have a great opportunity to educate the local and corporate HR and Purchasing teams on how to evaluate and select a staffing provider. Unlike direct-spend product purchases, temporary staffing contracts reflect factors controlled mainly by the buyer.

Since the employee pay rate is generally 80 percent of the bill rate, companies and their respective staffing vendors must first determine the target pay rate that will achieve the desired hiring profiles and retention goals. Then they need to agree on what benefits to offer to further support those objectives.

Managers at the local facility must retain the final decision-making ability because they know their facility the best. They understand how all the unique factors affect labor in their geographical location.

Companies also need to estimate the costs of a transition should they change staffing firms. Suppliers have the right to move their employees to another customer location, which can be extremely disruptive and costly.

As you design this contractual relationship, use the partial specification list on page 99 as a guide. By taking factors like these into account, you can greatly improve the outcome.

Please visit http://www.mau.com/casestudies to find in-depth, downloadable case studies of how MAU customers have outsourced noncore functions to increase efficiency and improve their bottom line.

Service Delivery Checklist

Company-Location Specific

- ❑ Compensation
- ❑ Benefits
- ❑ Market labor rates
- ❑ Turnover
- ❑ Absenteeism
- ❑ Product lines/cycles
- ❑ Management style
- ❑ Culture
- ❑ Disciplinary procedures
- ❑ Promotional opportunities
- ❑ Training requirements
- ❑ Union history/threat
- ❑ Shift models
- ❑ Contract labor ratios: temp/FTR
- ❑ Co-employment concerns
- ❑ EEOC claims history

Department Specific

- ❑ Supervisor styles
- ❑ Work rules
- ❑ Safety requirements
- ❑ Job duties

State and Region

- ❑ Labor laws: right to work
- ❑ Regulation: worker's comp
- ❑ Unemployment rates

City

- ❑ Population size
- ❑ Proximity to talent
- ❑ Educational level
- ❑ Labor availability

Staffing Services

- ❑ Screening and selection processes
  - ♦ Testing
  - ♦ Evaluation
- ❑ On boarding and assimilation
- ❑ Safety/risk management
- ❑ QC systems
- ❑ Management service expertise
  - ♦ Professional managers
  - ♦ First-line managers
  - ♦ Administrative
- ❑ Support hours offered
  - ♦ 24/7
  - ♦ 8/5
- ❑ On-time delivery guarantees

Transition of Suppliers

- ❑ Current-employee turnover
- ❑ New-employee orientation & training costs
- ❑ Loss of on-site management

About the Author

Since graduating from the University of Georgia in 1978, Randy has worked for MAU (Management, Analysis, and Utilization Inc.) a family-owned business founded by his father, William G. Hatcher Sr. When Randy joined the company, it had just seven full-time employees (including him, his brother, and father) and twenty-five temporary employees working at customer locations in Augusta, Georgia. Today, MAU's reach extends globally, and it is one of the largest private, minority-owned staffing and outsourcing firms in North America.

Randy has learned many lessons on his life journey. He has come to recognize that companies of the future will survive and flourish through their partnerships and that if businesses do not continue to reinvent themselves, they will fail or be commoditized. Most important to him is the value of operating a business under Godly principles.

A past member of the Young Presidents' Organization (YPO), Randy currently belongs to the World Presidents' Organization (WPO) and the Chief Executives' Organization (CEO).

His life passions include influencing behavior to encourage positive outcomes. In the business world, this aspiration has manifested itself through his pioneering roles in both the staffing and outsourcing industries, as well as through his many interactions with business leaders, whether one-on-one or in group settings. On the personal side, he enjoys teaching and stretching the minds of others to more deeply consider the tenets of the Christian faith.

Randy lives in Augusta, Georgia, with his wife, Marilee, and their twin Cairn terriers, Molly and Lucy.

About the Publisher

Pursuit Books seeks to challenge conventional thinking in the areas of business, family, and personal growth. We believe that as long as we're breathing, we all have room to grow and expand our minds in how we live in each of these spheres.

In business, it is unquestionably important to provide better and better products and service offerings. This entails the obvious ABCs of business, yet more than that, it demands a mind-set that creates, embraces, and implements the newest and best ideas and practices. Equally important is what happens in the lives of the people involved. Can you be a market leader and at the same time have a positive lifetime impact on your employees, their families, and those in the communities where you conduct business?

Perhaps the most hackneyed word we use today to describe families is "dysfunctional." By using it, we imply that some families actually exist without problems. Since Adam and Eve's family, everyone has struggled with dysfunction. No one humanly authored book can adequately address all the challenges any one family or marriage will face. At Pursuit Books, we promote new paths for learning how to improve relationships with loved ones and how to inspire others to do the same.

Lastly, but certainly not least, is how we can stretch ourselves in the area of personal growth. There is always an opportunity around the corner for each of us to grasp a bigger piece of the true pie of life: God's plan. To the degree each of us strives to live in faithfulness to His plan, our workplaces, our families, and the world will be better.

To all these ends, we seek authors whose works we can support and bring to you in the future. We welcome your feedback about our publications and any suggestions you might have about offerings we should consider. If we can help you in your life's journey, please contact us.